McKinsey Quarterly

2010 Number 4

This Quarter

It's easy to lose track of just how extraordinary the information technology and communications revolution we're living through is. This issue's lead article, "Clouds, big data, and smart assets: Ten tech-enabled business trends to watch," reminds us of how far technology still has to run; underscores its potential to reshape the nature of competition, strategy, and the enterprise itself; and highlights the emerging business opportunities.

Few if any organizations are truly prepared for the shifts described by the article's authors: Jacques Bughin, Michael Chui, and James Manyika. Yet there is no doubt some companies will get out ahead of them and create new competitive advantages that are both surprising and powerful. For a provocative picture of the business landscape that could result, read former Harvard Business School professor Shoshana Zuboff's article, "Creating value in the age of distributed capitalism." Zuboff argues that we are on the cusp of massive shifts in industry structure and that now is the time for executives to identify and harness forces that literally could destroy the boundaries of their businesses.

In a publishing industry itself experiencing great disruption, the *Quarterly* occupies an unusual place. Our mission is to help McKinsey & Company define the top-management agenda by shedding light on the biggest challenges facing senior executives. Doing so successfully is getting harder all the time in a world where leaders are continually bombarded by information. Over the past year, we've been listening to our readers through surveys and interviews and adapting our content to their changing needs. (We're also evolving our digital-distribution strategy and will share more on that in the months ahead.)

Senior executives say they want the *Quarterly* to shake up their thinking and then help them decide what to do in response. Accordingly, we've reoriented the "Leading Edge" section, at the front of the *Quarterly*, to highlight research, trends, and emerging ideas that should help executives view the world differently. We have also created a new department, "Applied Insight," to bottle up succinctly the tools and techniques our readers expect. To help our C-suite audience navigate our features more easily, we now provide quick summaries and greater variation in article lengths and formats.

What won't change is the depth and rigor our readers count on. In fact, we are committed to going deeper than ever on select topics by providing a rich constellation of perspectives from McKinsey consultants, practicing executives, academics, and other thought leaders. In this issue, for example, experts from Berkeley, Google, Microsoft, and Oxford weigh in on the technology trends outlined by our consultants in the cover story; and a moving, personal commentary from a senior executive on the source of her values illuminates new McKinsey research on centered leadership. The goal in all this work is to serve you better. We welcome your feedback as our evolution continues. o

Allen P. Webb

Allen P. Webb, Editor-in-Chief
Allen_Webb@McKinsey.com

On the cover

Features

Departments

Leading Edge

Applied Insight

On Our Web Site

Now available on
mckinseyquarterly.com

Global forces: An introduction

Five crucibles of change will restructure the world economy for the foreseeable future. In this video interview on our site, McKinsey director Peter Bisson explains the value of tracking global forces and how to build them into corporate strategy.

Other features:

Innovation and commercialization, 2010: McKinsey Global Survey results

After coping with the global economic crisis, companies are beginning to aim for growth again. But their approach to managing innovation and the challenges they face haven't changed. The survey results suggest a few ways to improve.

When companies underestimate low-cost rivals

Attackers are threatening premium players in market after market— and not only at the low end.

A better way to measure shop floor costs

Explore an interactive exhibit in which pathways and standardized manufacturing units reveal how costs vary when volumes or product mixes change.

Video and audio podcasts on iTunes

Download conversations with executives and authors in audio or video from iTunes.

audio: http://bit.ly/mckinseyitunesaudio
video: http://bit.ly/mckinseyitunesvideo

Join the *McKinsey Quarterly* community on Facebook

facebook.com/mckinseyquarterly

Follow us on Twitter

Receive notification of new content by following @McKQuarterly on Twitter.

Idea Exchange

Readers mix it up with authors of articles from *McKinsey Quarterly*
2010, Number 3

Global forces:
Five crucibles of innovation shaping global business

The cover package of the previous issue of *McKinsey Quarterly* examined five important trends likely to restructure and define the global economy for the foreseeable future. They are: the great rebalancing taking place as the center of economic growth shifts from developed to developing countries; the productivity imperative facing developed nations; and the growing importance of sustainability, the market state, and the global grid interconnecting economies.

Presented here are two parts of the conversation that appeared on mckinseyquarterly.com on some of these topics.

An unsustainable imbalance

Vignesh Babu
Bombardier Transportation, France

"The concept of 'designed in Europe/America, built in Asia' is being pursued by a number of companies, including my company, Bombardier. Yet despite the increasing quality of the workforce in China or India, the technologies and know-how for many engineering developments are still largely protected in the West. The seeds of innovation are far from being planted in the emerging markets, and it will be quite a long time before these jobs can be shipped to countries such as China and India."

McKinsey's Lowell Bryan responds:

"You're absolutely right that most of the highly skilled design roles remain in the developed world and that most of them will continue to be located there for the foreseeable future. Indeed, European and US multinational companies are in many ways thriving by continuing to employ very high-skilled labor in their home countries while outsourcing midlevel jobs to China and India. They can drive innovation from their home countries while saving labor costs.

"Unfortunately, the missing jobs are a major contributor to the structural-unemployment issues that the European and US economies face. These issues also contribute, therefore, to the related structural fiscal deficits in Europe and the United States, since out-of-work people are paid entitlements and have no income to tax. Over the medium term, these kinds of critical global imbalances are not sustainable."

Scared or salivating?

Greg Hoxley

Technology and innovation manager, Sinclair Knight Merz,
Melbourne, Australia

"Less than 50 percent of the executives you surveyed feel that the
effects on profits will be positive. How can this be? These forces are
going to provide enormous disruptive change over the next decade,
and accompanying this change will be opportunity. The apparently
negative view of the outcomes misses a chance to grasp and shape
these forces and gain an advantage. A very interesting insight into
the mind-set of those surveyed."

McKinsey's Elizabeth Stephenson responds:
"Mr. Hoxley, you are right that the coming decade will offer significant
opportunity—but not for everyone. How one views that future seems to
depend on one's position in it. A deeper dive into our survey data
suggests that a company's geographic location may explain much of the
difference between executives who are running scared and those who
are salivating at new growth opportunities. Executives in faster-growing
economies, for example, are more likely to be optimistic. Seventy-
seven percent of respondents in the Asia-Pacific region answered that
'the shift of economic activity between and within regions' will have
a positive impact on the profitability of their companies over the next five
years, compared with just 43 percent in North America, where the
impact of the global recession was more pronounced.

"Furthermore, when questioning executives on the impact of the 'great
rebalancing' that's occurring as economic activity shifts from developed
to emerging markets, we found significant differences in responses
by sector and by overall business strategy. Executives in high tech and
manufacturing were more positive than those in energy or finance.
And, predictably, those who said their companies' strategic decision-
making processes 'emphasize long-term fundamentals' were
more optimistic than those in companies more preoccupied with short-
term challenges."

Visit **mckinseyquarterly.com** to share your
own comments or see more from our readers on these
and other topics.

A truer picture of China's export machine

John Horn, Vivien Singer, and Jonathan Woetzel

China's growth depends less on exports than conventional wisdom suggests. Perhaps it's time to double down on the Chinese consumer.

Is China's economic growth largely dependent on exports, or is it becoming more domestically led? That's a question economists are vigorously debating—and an important one for policy makers and executives alike. An increasingly consumption- and investment-focused Chinese economy could improve the chances of more balanced trading relationships with developed economies. At the same time, businesses operating in China or planning to enter it could find greater opportunities as the economy accelerated its transition from a manufacturing center to a key consumer market.

To shed light on this question, we developed a new way of measuring the role of export growth in China's overall economic expansion. We found that exports have been a major driver, but not one as dominant as commonly believed. Indeed, there are clear signs that a shift toward domestically driven economic growth is well under way. The picture that emerges of the Chinese economy has implications for the growth and supply chain strategies of businesses in China and elsewhere.[1]

A different way to measure exports

Arguments over the true nature of China's economic reliance on exports have been rooted in the difficulty of appropriately measuring the export sector. The traditional measure governments and most analysts use is the growth of total exports as a share of GDP growth. This measure indicates that export growth has accounted, on average, for almost 40 percent of the total growth in real GDP since 1990—rising to almost 60 percent since 2000.[2]

Yet these numbers, portraying a dominant and growing role of exports, are at odds with the fact that China was one of the few countries that escaped the great 2008–09 global downturn without a major economic slowdown—suggesting that internal growth played an important role. That's one reason

There are clear signs that a shift to domestically driven economic growth is well under way.

other economists have used a very different measure: growth in net exports (total exports minus total imports) as a share of GDP growth. By that metric, exports contributed only between 10 and 20 percent of China's annual 10 percent GDP growth in recent years.

We contend that both measures are misleading. Using total exports neglects the fact that many of China's export shipments include a fair number of imported goods that are reassembled, combined with domestic content, or otherwise modified before being exported. Failing to remove these imports from the total export figure overstates how much value exports contribute to GDP. On the other hand, a strict net export measure (exports minus imports) underestimates the contribution of exports to GDP, because many imports *aren't* used in assembly and exported but rather sold to Chinese consumers and businesses.

We calculated a measure we call domestic value-added exports (DVAE) to assess more accurately the role of exports in GDP growth. DVAE is what you get after subtracting from total exports *only* those imports used in the production of goods and services that are subsequently exported. In automobiles, for example, finished imports are not subtracted from our measure of exports. But engine parts imported to manufacture motor bikes for export would be.

Governments usually don't break out total imports into those used domestically (for production, investment, and consumption) and those used for exports, and China is no exception. So we estimated the country's DVAE by using data from three different sources, each with its own strengths and limitations. The results were remarkably consistent—and collectively shed a powerful light on the evolution of supply chain strategies, Chinese consumption,

and Chinese economic performance during the global downturn (see sidebar, "About the research").

Supply chain shifts

On average, our analysis suggests that imported goods accounted for 40 to 55 percent of the value of total exports from 2002 to 2008. Put another way, roughly half of China's exports represent domestic value added. Concurrently, DVAE's share of exports generally has risen over time, suggesting that China has become less of a pure assembler of imported goods—a publicly stated government policy goal.

That has implications for many companies' supply chains and business models. If your company is a manufacturer in China that is primarily processing intermediate components for reexport—a

Exhibit 1

Traditional measures overestimate the contribution of exports to China's GDP growth.

Growth in real exports[1] as % of GDP growth

■ Total exports   ■ Domestic value-added exports (DVAE)[2]

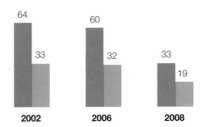

	2002	2006	2008
Total exports	64	60	33
DVAE	33	32	19

[1]Growth in China slowed in 2008 to 8.9% (on an expenditure basis), from 12.9% in 2007, while global growth declined to 1.9%, from 4%, with negative growth in the 4th quarter—the beginning of the global recession.
[2]DVAE = total exports minus those imports used in the production of goods and services that are subsequently exported; calculated as average of values, using data available for given year: 51% of total exports in 2002, 53% in 2006, 57% in 2008.

Source: China Customs data; Robert Koopman, Zhi Wang, and Shang-Jin Wei, "How much of Chinese exports is really made in China? Assessing foreign and domestic value-added in gross exports," US International Trade Commission, Office of Economics, working paper, March 2008

Exhibit 2

Since 2007, the contribution of exports to overall growth has declined dramatically.

Decomposition of GDP growth, %

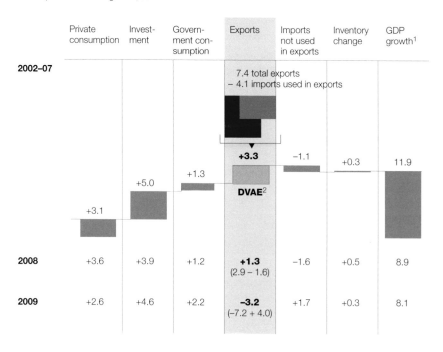

	Private consumption	Invest-ment	Govern-ment con-sumption	Exports	Imports not used in exports	Inventory change	GDP growth[1]
2002–07	+3.1	+5.0	+1.3	7.4 total exports − 4.1 imports used in exports **+3.3** DVAE[2]	−1.1	+0.3	11.9
2008	+3.6	+3.9	+1.2	**+1.3** (2.9 − 1.6)	−1.6	+0.5	8.9
2009	+2.6	+4.6	+2.2	**−3.2** (−7.2 + 4.0)	+1.7	+0.3	8.1

[1] Calculated on expenditure basis; figures may differ from those based on industry value added, depending in part on updates released by Chinese government.
[2] Domestic value-added exports (DVAE) = total exports minus those imports used in the production of goods and services that are subsequently exported.

Source: Robert Koopman, Zhi Wang, and Shang-Jin Wei, "How much of Chinese exports is really made in China? Assessing foreign and domestic value-added in gross exports," US International Trade Commission, Office of Economics, working paper, March 2008

Taiwan-based original-design manufacturer (ODM) of household goods, for example—it's probably time to consider alternative locations for the assembly work. With China moving up the value chain and beginning to export more skill-intensive goods and services, chances are that pure assembly will soon be less costly in other parts of Asia.

Exports, consumption, and strategy

We also applied our DVAE analysis to reassess the contribution of exports to GDP growth in the years for which we have overlapping data among our three metrics. We found that China's export sector contributed 19 to 33 percent of total GDP growth between 2002 and 2008 (Exhibit 1). That's only about half of the export contribution

About the research

To estimate domestic value-added exports (DVAE), we took three approaches, using data from three different sources. First, we applied a sector-based approach, using data from IHS Global Insight, which provided Chinese import data for more than 30 industries. We classified them as industries producing finished goods (such as food and beverages), intermediate products (industrial chemicals, for example), or raw materials (such as the mining industry). We then assumed that all intermediate products and raw materials were used for creating exports, while none of the finished-goods industries accounted for exports.

The second approach applied input–output measures at the industry level, using data from a working paper from the US International Trade Commission's Office of Economics.[1] The third metric came from China's official customs data on reexports—products whose parts are imported, assembled, and then exported. We assumed that all such reexports were made from imported goods, while all other exports were made from domestic content only. Removing the reexports left us with our third proxy for DVAE.

[1]Robert Koopman, Zhi Wang, and Shang-Jin Wei, "How much of Chinese exports is really made in China? Assessing foreign and domestic value-added in gross exports," US International Trade Commission, Office of Economics, working paper, March 2008.

indicated by traditional total-exports measures.[3]

In other words, DVAE analysis suggests that exports have been an important driver of China's growth, but not the dominant one, and that most common wisdom over-estimates the role of exports while underestimating the role of domestic consumption for China's growth. Any Chinese or multi-national company that currently manufactures goods in China and primarily exports them to other countries should ask itself whether it needs to scale up its domestic strategy to get a bigger piece of the pie. This involves developing a more granular understanding of the Chinese market, making products that appeal to the Chinese consumer, and finding ways to market and distribute them effectively—all while contending with increasingly formidable Chinese competitors.[4]

China's 'downturn' and the road ahead

A comparison between DVAE's contribution to growth and that of other major macroeconomic components shows that DVAE topped private consumption, but was less important than investment, over the 2002–07 period (Exhibit 2). In the downturn years, 2008 and 2009,[5] exports contributed much less to growth than other factors did, which explains why the Chinese economy could not fully match its GDP growth rates in the earlier part of the decade. However, the shift to a greater role for private consumption, investment, and finished imports explains how China could weather the downturn well and indicates movement toward a domestically focused economy, even though exports will probably continue to play an important role when the global economy picks up.

Of course, continued changes in the value of the renminbi in the coming years will also affect the evolution of Chinese trade. The more value-added-focused export sector suggested by our DVAE analysis implies that a greater share of exports will consist of higher-priced goods that compete more directly with those of developed nations. That, coupled with an appreciating Chinese currency, points to the creation of more balanced trading partnerships with the rest of the world—and an important shift in context when businesses consider future strategic moves in China. ○

[1] In this article, we address only national GDP, not employment or regional effects within China. Our interest is the overall health of the Chinese economy, and we leave aside the question of which groups or regions are better off because of any changes in the overall level of exports.
[2] Calculated from the McKinsey Global Institute (MGI) China urbanization model.
[3] Not surprising, exports measured by domestic value-added exports (DVAE) contributed more—almost two times more—to GDP growth than exports measured on a net basis. DVAE therefore represents a middle ground between total- and net-export measures.
[4] See Jeff Galvin, Jimmy Hexter, and Martin Hirt, "Building a second home in China," mckinseyquarterly.com, June 2010; and Yuval Atsmon et al., "2009 Annual Chinese Consumer Study, Part II: One Country, Many Markets—Targeting the Chinese Consumer with McKinsey *ClusterMap*," McKinsey Insights China, September 2009.
[5] The DVAE for 2009 is based on data from IHS Global Insight only.

John Horn is a consultant in McKinsey's Washington, DC, office; **Vivien Singer** is a consultant with the McKinsey Global Institute; and **Jonathan Woetzel** is a director in the Shanghai office.

Riding Asia's digital tiger

Vikash Daga, Nimal Manuel, and Laxman Narasimhan

Asia is the world's hottest area of Internet growth, but the dynamics on the ground vary widely by nation.

Asia's emerging markets are poised for explosive digital growth. The region's two largest economies—China and India—already boast some 500 million Internet users, and we forecast nearly 700 million more will be added by 2015. Other emerging Asian nations have the potential to grow at a similarly torrid pace. We estimate that within five years, this billion-plus user market may generate revenues of more than $80 billion in Internet commerce, access fees, device sales, and so forth.

To better understand the consumers, growth prospects, and problems, we surveyed more than 13,000 individuals across China, India, and Malaysia—countries at very different stages of their digital evolution.[1] The key finding? While there were some notable differences in the types of content consumers favor and the devices they use, significant demand is waiting to be unlocked in all three nations. That could lead to growing markets for digital content and services and to new opportunities around digital marketing, including efforts to reach consumers via Internet sales channels.

Malaysia

Of the three markets we researched, Malaysia is the most advanced. While the country has only around 15 million–plus Internet users, that's close to 55 percent of the total population, and mobile Internet penetration is close to 30 percent of it. Given the Malaysian government's push to expand high-speed broadband, we forecast that the country will have up to 25 million Internet users by 2015, or close to 80 percent of the population. As both fixed and wireless broadband grow, we project that more than 50 percent of all users will choose to have both personal-computer and mobile-device options for getting online.

Malaysians consume 35 percent more digital media than Internet users in China and 150 percent more than users in India, particularly on social-networking sites and instant messaging. That may, for example, give handset manufacturers opportunities to build social-network access into their devices. We also found that Malaysians like to multitask across both digital and traditional media. For advertisers, that's problematic, since viewers are paying less attention to traditional media content—and thus advertising.

China

China leads the world in sheer numbers of Internet users—more than 420 million people, or close to 30 percent of the population. Over 80 percent surf the Web from home, while 230 million use mobile devices. We forecast that the number of Internet users will almost double over the next five years, hitting 770 million people, or 55 percent of the population. More than 70 percent will use both PCs and handheld devices.

China's digital usage, which is similar to that of the United States, skews toward instant messaging, social networks, gaming, and streaming video. Increasingly, Internet users in China are substituting digital media for traditional ones, with

Over the next five years, nearly 700 million more Asians will start using the Internet.

Penetration,[1] millions of users

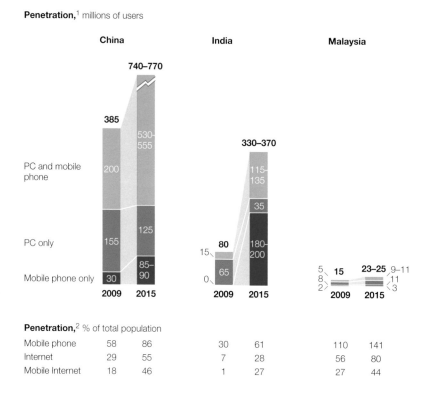

Penetration,[2] % of total population	China 2009	China 2015	India 2009	India 2015	Malaysia 2009	Malaysia 2015
Mobile phone	58	86	30	61	110	141
Internet	29	55	7	28	56	80
Mobile Internet	18	46	1	27	27	44

[1] Figures for 2015 are projected.
[2] Penetration above 100% indicates some users have multiple connected devices.

the potential for further cannibal-ization as digital consumption grows. This development has stark implications for advertisers and how they allocate future marketing budgets. Consumers, meanwhile, also use the Internet in their purchasing decisions. They are more influenced by recommendations from social-network contacts and friends than by traditional marketing messages or visits to company Web sites.

India

With only 7 percent of the population connected (81 million users), India is Asia's digital sleeper. Yet we believe that it's poised to become a truly mobile-Internet society as new users leapfrog PCs altogether. We project that by 2015, the number of Internet users will increase almost fivefold, to more than 350 million—28 percent of the population—with more than half of those accessing the Web via mobile phones. To capture this opportunity, companies will need to roll out wired and wireless broadband networks aggressively, to make smartphones and network access more affordable, and to develop new content types.

Consumer demand clearly is robust. On average, Indians spend more than four hours a day consuming on-line and offline content. On PCs, often used in cyber cafés, Indians spend much time e-mailing and are heavy consumers of downloaded videos and music, as well as DVD movies. While Indian consumers use mobile phones predominantly for voice services, they also treat them

Internet opportunities in emerging Asia could reach approximately $80 billion by 2015.

Revenues,[1] $ billion

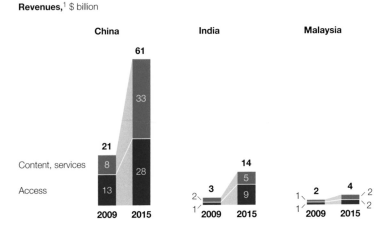

[1] Figures for 2015 are projected.

as offline personal-entertainment devices, listening to radio stations or to downloaded music. There is significant pent-up demand for more convenient and personalized Internet access—a void the mobile Web could fill.

Embracing the opportunity

High hardware costs, inconsistent network quality, and limited access could check these optimistic growth prospects. But the extent of such barriers varies by nation, and there's notable progress overcoming them. Construction of network infrastructure is proceeding apace— companies in India, for example, just spent nearly $25 billion on tele- communications spectrum. Mean- while, hardware and access costs are declining in most markets. The biggest challenge is to make money while creating a variety of low-cost content. Three issues are especially important:

Innovators and entrepreneurs must develop content creation and delivery models priced low enough to compete against the pirated options currently available.

Content and Web services providers need to foster the growth of local and regional advertising markets to help defray the cost of content creation.

E-commerce platforms, includ- ing transaction systems that make purchases more convenient and trusted, must be developed.

At the same time, companies in consumer-facing sectors (for instance, automotive, packaged consumer goods, and retailing) will need to reconsider their marketing and advertising strategies in light of the shift away from traditional media. At stake is a significant competitive advantage in a region that already boasts more than half the world's Internet users—and will only continue to grow. ○

[1] Field surveys were conducted across 50 cities and in-depth ethnographic profiles developed to form a cross-device, longi- tudinal view of how the region's digital con- sumption is evolving.

The authors wish to acknowledge the contributions of Nal Gollagunta to this article.

Vikash Daga is a principal in McKinsey's Delhi office, where **Laxman Narasimhan** is a director; **Nimal Manuel** is a principal in the Kuala Lumpur office.

Digital marketing's new vocabulary

David Edelman and Brian Salsberg

The impact of "hijacked" and "sold" media could rival that of traditional advertising.

New types of media are challenging the strategies, structures, and operations of many marketing organizations. The resulting changes are so profound that all senior executives should understand them—or risk losing touch with their customers.

Case in point: the popular "paid, owned, earned" framework, which marketers have adopted in recent years to distinguish different ways of interacting with consumers, financing those interactions, and measuring their performance, increasingly appears too limited. We believe two new types of media— "sold" and "hijacked"—must be added, and together they have the potential to affect brands and shareholder value much as traditional advertising has.

Paid media include traditional advertising and similar vehicles: a company pays for space or for a third party to promote its products. This market is far from dying; options for marketers are expanding exponentially with the emergence of more targeted cable TV programming, online display placement, and other channels, not to mention online videos and search engine marketing, which are attracting greater interest.

Owned media consist of properties or channels owned by the company that uses them for marketing purposes (such as catalogs, Web sites, Facebook fan pages, retail stores, and e-mail alert programs that notify customers of special offers).

Earned media are generated when consumers use their own "media" to promote a company's products and content at no cost to itself. Honda Japan, for example, undertook a promotion on the social-networking site Mixi, where more than 630,000 people registered for information about the launch of its new CR-Z vehicle. The company automatically added "CR-Z" to these users' Mixi login names (for example, "Taro CR-Z") and gave them a chance to win a car. Non-registered users wondered why people suddenly had login names incorporating CR-Z. Thanks to the buzz, prelaunch orders reached 4,500 units, and actual sales topped 10,000 units in the first month.

Sold media are formed when one marketer's *owned* media become another's *paid* media—for instance, when an e-commerce retailer sells ad space on its Web site. We define such sold media as owned media whose traffic is so strong that other organizations place their content or e-commerce engines within that environment. Johnson & Johnson, for example, has created BabyCenter, a stand-alone media property that promotes the company's products and even those of its competitors. Besides generating income, the presence of other marketers makes the site seem objective, offers companies the opportunity to learn valuable information about the appeal of competitors' marketing, and may help expand user traffic at the Web sites of all participating companies.

Hijacked media, the opposite of earned media, involve an asset or campaign that's held hostage by consumers, other stakeholders, or activists who make negative allegations about a brand or product. Members of social-networking sites, for instance, are learning that they can voice their opinions quickly, visibly, and in very damaging ways—in essence, hijacking media to apply pressure on the businesses that created them. In many of these cases, such as a prank online video of two Domino's Pizza employees contaminating sandwiches,[1] the negative impact was instant, gained momentum as the content went viral, and required tremendous effort to mitigate the damage to the target company's reputation. Only now are companies realizing the ramifications of hijacked media—and the fact that no response can be sufficiently quick or thoughtful once they are unleashed.

> Marketers may be on the front line for delivering quality, but the entire organization must recognize the importance of fulfilling consumer standards for consistency, utility, and the proper use of information.

An extended view across all evolving forms of media, now including sold and hijacked ones, isn't relevant just for marketers. As quality standards, investment dollars, and the strategic focus on emerging media all rise, an organization's entire senior team should broaden its discussion to include building the company's brand. At one consumer electronics company, for example, the CEO requires all business unit executives, not just marketing managers, to develop explicit strategies for how they will use these new forms of media to gain a competitive advantage. It's not just a brainstorming exercise: people are now exposed to products and brands on so many fronts that the business of forging relationships with consumers can't be delegated purely to the marketing department. Every customer interaction—in a traditional retail setting, online, or through marketing messages—presents not only an opportunity for a deeper relationship but also risks. Executives across the organization need to be both informed and involved.

That's why forward-thinking companies recognize that a consumer's perception of their brands is tied not only to products but also to the experience consumers have with all types of media. Marketers may be on the front line for delivering quality, but the entire organization must recognize the importance of fulfilling consumer standards for consistency, utility, and the proper use of information. Nike, for example, is a master of meeting this high bar of expectations through a bevy of owned-media channels, which deliver experiences that form a tight bond between consumers and the company's athletic equipment. More companies should use the full range of media channels at their disposal to differentiate their brands. That should be a priority for the senior team. o

[1] Stephanie Clifford, "Video prank at Domino's taints brand," *New York Times*, April 15, 2009.

David Edelman is a principal in McKinsey's Boston office, and **Brian Salsberg** is a principal in the Tokyo office.

The full version of this article is available on mckinseyquarterly.com.

Thinking beyond the public company

Robert E. Wright

Mutuals and partnerships were once the ownership structures of choice for many enterprises. Should they be again?

Policy debates about business reforms invariably rely on one big assumption: the basic mechanism of the public company has malfunctioned, and corrective regulation will help safeguard the interests of shareholders and the public. Look no further than the current financial-reform bill, with its plethora of new rules aimed at correcting incentive mismatches that led to excessive risk taking at big, publicly traded Wall Street firms. Or the debates on health care reform, where the initial political impulse was to impose a government option to rein in "greedy" publicly traded health insurers.

An emphasis on regulating the behavior of public companies is understandable: their steady spread across the US business landscape since the 18th century, partly in response to the capital demands of widespread industrialization, conveys an impression that they are the natural form for large enterprises. Yet throughout much of modern corporate history, other ownership structures, such as mutuals, partnerships, and cooperatives, also played a prominent role, coexisting with the joint stock company. These structures represent an alternative for tailoring ownership and governance to the risks and operating profiles of specific economic sectors. They might offer regulators cheaper and more effective ways of limiting financial crises and industry implosions. Some entrepreneurs may even find them a better way to raise capital and manage the risks of new businesses.

The financial-services industry is a stunning example of recent and dramatic change in the prevailing corporate form. From the 18th century up through at least 1970, many savings and loans, investment banks, and insurance companies were organized as mutuals, partnerships, or joint stock–mutual hybrids (exhibit). The business models of insurers (fire, health, life, livestock, and marine) and of savings institutions (savings banks and societies, savings and loans) were characterized by long-term contracts and asymmetries

Starting around 1970, joint stock companies surged across much of the US financial-services landscape.

 Mutual/hybrid[1]
 Joint stock

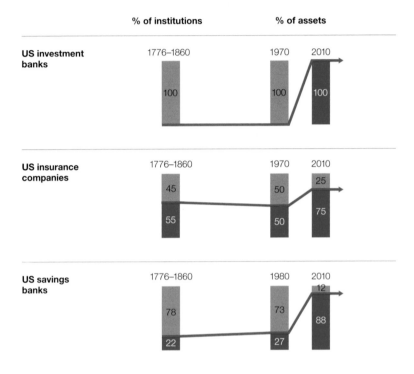

[1] For investment banks: partnership.

Source: for savings banks: Lawrence R. Cordell, Gregor D. MacDonald, and Mark E. Wohar, "Corporate ownership and the thrift crisis," *Journal of Law and Economics*, 1993, Volume 32, Number 2, pp. 719–56; for insurance companies: George Zanjani, "Regulation, capital, and the evolution of the organizational form in US life insurance," *American Economic Review*, 2007, Volume 97, Number 3, pp. 973–83; for investment banks: Alan D. Morrison and William J. Wilhelm, Jr., "The demise of investment-banking partnerships: Theory and evidence," working paper, July 2004

between what proprietors and customers knew about the risks of doing business with one another. These conditions were well suited to mutual charters stipulating that customers should own the organization and often entrusting their aggregated interests to independent sales agents.

Similarly, policy makers in the late 18th and the 19th centuries forced many mercantile houses, broker–dealers, and investment banks to remain partnerships or sole proprietorships.[1] They worried about "agency costs" in these businesses: skilled salaried managers with good information could defraud their companies, customers, and shareholders by trading on their own account and engaging in other forms of self-dealing. To keep the incentives of such firms aligned with those of society, managers had to be owners, and their ownership stakes had to be illiquid and constitute a large percentage of their net worth.

These views remained accepted wisdom until recently. In the 1970s and '80s, however, mutuals lost their grip on the savings-and-loan and insurance industries, and by 2005 all the major US investment banks had gone public. This phenomenon was not confined to the United States. British building societies, for example, demutualized thanks to regulatory changes pursued by the Conservative governments of the 1980s. The transition's causes, too complex to detail here, are no doubt related to largely positive shifts—toward a world of more liberal markets, more deeply integrated global financial systems, and faster, cheaper communications and information processing.

Yet subsequent challenges, including the US savings-and-loan crisis of the 1980s and the global financial crisis of 2008, raise the question of unintended consequences. The recently passed US financial-reform act suggests that there's little appetite among policy makers for a broad restoration of organizational diversity. But more limited goals may be useful. Policy makers looking for sustainable ways to contain agency problems in the finance industry, for example, could design incentives that promote mutuals or partnerships when public companies divest units or form joint ventures. Life and property-and-casualty insurers that have struggled as joint stock companies could remutualize.

Private equity—which at its best is rooted in the beneficial alliance of management incentives and investor interests—also could play a role in encouraging diverse ownership structures. And at the grassroots level, would-be microfinanciers and community bankers should seriously consider mutual forms, such as credit unions, that accommodate social goals more readily than joint stock companies do. Modest steps such as these toward a broader portfolio of organizational forms might help rebalance risk and reward in these volatile times. ○

[1] Robert E. Wright, "Corporate entrepreneurship in the antebellum South," in Susanna Delfino, Michele Gillespie, and Louis Kyriakoudes, eds., *The Transformations of Southern Society, 1790–1860*, Columbia, MO: University of Missouri Press, 2011.

Robert Wright is the Nef Family Chair of Political Economy at Augustana College, in South Dakota, and the author of *Fubarnomics: A Lighthearted, Serious Look at America's Economic Ills* (Prometheus, 2010).

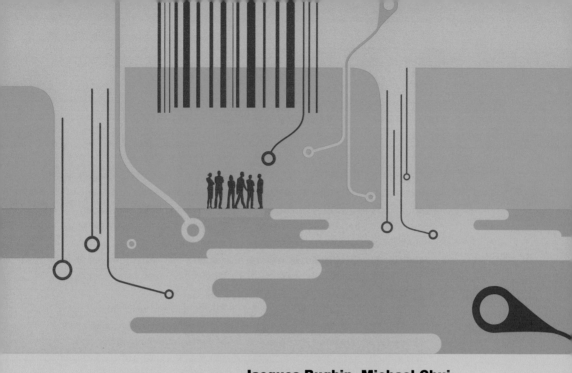

Jacques Bughin, Michael Chui, and James Manyika

Clouds, big data, and smart assets:

Ten tech-enabled business trends to watch

Technological shifts are upending traditional business models. To stay ahead of the curve, executives must reimagine how their organizations create and deliver products and services.

With commentary from:

William Dutton
Director of the Oxford Internet
Institute, University of Oxford

Kris Pister
Professor of electrical engineering
and computer sciences,
University of California, Berkeley

Hal Varian
Chief economist, Google

Rob Bernard
Chief environmental strategist,
Microsoft

Rob Salkowitz
Author of *Young World Rising:
How Youth, Technology, and
Entrepreneurship Are Changing the
World from the Bottom Up*

The technology landscape is evolving at a dizzying pace. Facebook, in just over two short years, has quintupled in size to a network that touches more than 500 million users. More than 4 billion people around the world now use cell phones, and for 450 million of those people the Web is a fully mobile experience. The ways information technologies are deployed are changing too, as new developments such as virtualization and cloud computing reallocate technology costs and usage patterns while creating new ways for individuals to consume goods and services and for entrepreneurs and enterprises to dream up viable business models.

We've attempted to distill the implications of these and many other profound changes underway as a set of ten technology-enabled business trends.[1] Not only are they reshaping strategy across a wide swath of industries, they are spawning new ways to manage talent and assets, as well as catalyzing fresh thinking about organizational structures. Exploiting these trends typically doesn't fall to any one executive—and as change accelerates, the odds of missing a beat rise significantly. So merely understanding the ten trends outlined here isn't enough for senior executives. They also must devise a management approach that will help their organizations meet these new demands.

For the first six trends, which can be applied across an enterprise, it will be important to assign the responsibility for identifying the specific implications of each issue to functional groups and business units. The impact of these six trends—distributed cocreation, networks as organizations, deeper collaboration, the Internet of Things, experimentation with big data, and wiring for a sustainable world—often will vary considerably in different parts of the organization and should be managed accordingly. But local accountability won't be sufficient. Because some of the most powerful applications of these trends will cut across traditional organizational boundaries, senior leaders should catalyze regular collisions among teams in different corners of the company that are wrestling with similar issues.

Three of the trends—anything-as-a-service, multisided business models, and innovation from the bottom of the pyramid—augur far-reaching changes in the business environment that could require radical shifts in strategy. CEOs and their immediate senior teams need to grapple with these issues; otherwise it will be too difficult to generate the interdisciplinary, enterprise-wide insights needed to exploit these trends fully. Once opportunities start emerging, senior executives also need to turn their organizations into laboratories capable of quickly testing and learning on a small scale and then expand successes quickly. And finally, the tenth trend, using technology to improve communities and

[1] The ten trends described in this article build on eight we examined in an article from 2007. For more, see James M. Manyika, Roger P. Roberts, and Kara L. Sprague, "Eight business technology trends to watch," mckinseyquarterly.com, December 2007. Those eight trends have continued to spread (though often at a more rapid pace than we anticipated), morph in unexpected ways, and grow in number to an even ten.

generate societal benefits by linking citizens, requires action by not just senior business executives but also leaders in government, non-governmental organizations, and citizens.

Across the board, the stakes are high. Consider the results of a recent *McKinsey Quarterly* survey of global executives[2] on the impact that participatory Web 2.0 technologies (such as social networks, wikis, and microblogs) have on management and performance. The survey found that deploying these technologies to create networked organizations that foster innovative collaboration among employees, customers, and business partners is highly correlated with market share gains. That's just one example of how these trends transcend technology and provide a map of the terrain for creating value and competing effectively in these challenging and uncertain times.

Distributed cocreation moves into the mainstream

In the past few years, the ability to organize communities of Web participants to develop, market, and support products and services has moved from the margins of business practice to the mainstream. Wikipedia and a handful of open-source software developers were the pioneers. But in signs of the steady march forward, 70 percent of the executives we recently surveyed[3] said that their companies regularly created value through Web communities. Similarly, more than 68 million bloggers post reviews and recommendations about products and services.

Intuit is among the companies that use the Web to extend their reach and lower the cost of serving customers. For example, it hosts customer support communities for its financial and tax return products, where more experienced customers can offer advice and support to those who need help. The most significant contributors become visible to the community by showing the number of questions they have answered and the number of "thanks" they have received from other users. By our estimates, when customer communities handle an issue, the per-contact cost can be as low as 10 percent of the cost to resolve the issue through traditional call centers.

Facebook has marshaled its community for product development. The leading social network recently recruited 300,000 users to translate its site into 70 languages—the translation for its French-language site

---

[2]"How Web 2.0 is helping companies compete: McKinsey Global Survey results," to be published in the fall of 2010 on mckinseyquarterly.com.
[3]"How companies are benefiting from Web 2.0: McKinsey Global Survey results," mckinseyquarterly.com, September 2009.

took just one day. The community continues to translate updates and new modules.

Yet for every success in tapping communities to create value, there are still many failures. Some companies neglect the up-front research needed to identify potential participants who have the right skill sets and will be motivated to participate over the longer term. Since cocreation is a two-way process, companies must also provide feedback to stimulate continuing participation and commitment. Getting incentives right is important as well: cocreators often value reputation more than money. Finally, an organization must gain a high level of trust within a Web community to earn the engagement of top participants.

Making the network the organization

In earlier research, we noted that the Web was starting to force open the boundaries of organizations, allowing nonemployees to offer their expertise in novel ways. Now many companies are pushing substantially beyond that starting point, building and managing flexible networks that extend across internal and often even external borders. The recession underscored the value of such flexibility in managing volatility. We believe that the more porous, networked organizations of the future will need to organize work around critical tasks rather than molding it to constraints imposed by corporate structures.

Dow Chemical set up a social network to help managers identify the talent they need to execute projects across different business units and functions. To broaden the pool of talent, Dow has even extended the network to include former employees, such as retirees. Other companies are using networks to tap external talent pools. These networks include online labor markets (such as Amazon.com's Mechanical Turk) and contest services (such as Innocentive and Zooppa) that help solve business problems.

Management orthodoxies still prevent most companies from leveraging talent beyond full-time employees who are tied to existing organizational structures. Pilot programs that connect individuals across organizational boundaries are a good way to experiment with new models, but incentive structures must be overhauled and role models established to make these programs succeed. In the longer term, networked organizations will focus on the orchestration of tasks rather than the "ownership" of workers.

Collaboration at scale

Collaboration technologies that promise to improve the efficiency and effectiveness of knowledge workers are on the rise. Wikis and blogs have gone mainstream, and growth rates of video and Web conferencing are expected to top 20 percent annually over the next few years.

In one noteworthy example, the US intelligence community made wikis, documents, and blogs available to analysts across agencies (with appropriate security controls, of course). The result was a greater exchange of information within and among agencies and faster access to expertise in the intelligence community. Engineering company Bechtel established a centralized, open-collaboration database of design and engineering information to support global projects. Engineers starting new ones found that the database, which contained up to 25 percent of the material they needed, lowered launch costs and sped up times to completion.

For technology to be effective, organizations first need a better understanding of how knowledge work actually takes place. A good starting point is to map the informal pathways through which information travels, how employees interact, and where wasteful bottlenecks lie. The next leap forward in the productivity of knowledge workers will come from interactive technologies combined with complementary investments in process innovations and training. Strategic choices, such as whether to extend collaboration networks to customers and suppliers, will be critical.

Commentary
William Dutton | Director of the Oxford Internet Institute, University of Oxford

The degree to which individuals can control the patterns in which they network with other people—within and outside organizations—is the biggest change afoot in companies. It's empowering a revolution comparable to the one that put PCs on the map, in the early 1980s.

The Internet allows individuals to build informal networks within and beyond the organization: to understand who should be communicating with whom. This is a dramatic change that will enable companies to move decision making nearer to the ground level, empowering individuals closer to the customer or the service. Thus, the people best informed about a particular topic or activity become involved in the discussion. Collaborative organizations enabled by Internet technologies also will allow people to mine distributed intelligence within and beyond organizations. This ability of individuals to network outside institutions expands the boundaries of the firm.

Many organizations aren't thinking about the networked individual. They're still focused on their own organizational systems and traditional institutional networks. They may be a bit confused, and there is a tendency for organizations to be reactionary or even protectionist about what they don't understand. Rather than put up walls, managers need to get involved in collaborative networks so that they can better understand them and capture their value for the organization.

The growing 'Internet of Things'

Assets themselves are becoming elements of an information system, with the ability to capture, compute, communicate, and collaborate around information—something that has come to be known as the "Internet of Things." Embedded with sensors, actuators, and communications capabilities, such objects will soon be able to absorb and transmit information on a massive scale and, in some cases, to adapt and react to changes in the environment automatically. These "smart" assets can make processes more efficient, give products new capabilities, and spark novel business models.

Earlier this year in the *Quarterly*, we described in detail the early impact of the Internet of Things: sensors in vehicles that help insurers set prices and drivers avoid accidents; sensors in patients that help physicians modify treatments rapidly; sensors in factories that automatically adjust operations; and the like. The range of possible applications and their business impact have yet to be fully explored, however. Applications that improve process and energy efficiency (see trend number six, "Wiring for a sustainable world") may be good starting points for trials, since the number of successful installations in these areas is growing. For more complex applications, laboratory experiments, small-scale pilots, and partnerships with early technology adopters may be more fruitful, less risky approaches.

Commentary

Kris Pister | Professor at the University of California, Berkeley, and originator of the term "smart dust," which refers to wireless networks of millimeter-scale sensor nodes

The Internet of Things is no longer about, "Does this stuff really work?" Rather, it's about figuring out the best strategy and the best business case in which to use it. I didn't think the first place that smart dust would find a commercial home would be in industrial automation. But that has been a home run. Wireless-sensor products are being used in oil refineries, paper mills, chemical processing, and wastewater treatment, improving productivity and safety and reducing downtime.

Meanwhile, the "smart grid" is just getting started. Soon, there will be sensors on every part of it: fuel exploration and generation (where they already are installed) all the way through transmission, distribution, and use. There are already dozens, if not hundreds, of sensors in your car and in trucks and buses. Today, they are all wired, but it's likely this technology will go wireless, as will the monitoring of supply chains—all with huge increases in visibility and efficiency.

What could truly change things is the real-time location capability that the next generation of wireless sensors will provide. The location-based services and location awareness of cell phones and other technologies are about to expand ten- or even a thousandfold. This will allow the merging of existing Web databases with location information from your cell phone, weather information, and historical data from wireless sensors. All of this will be collected and put together to provide answers that are not all that intuitively obvious, such as finding a parking space. Once you start mining all of this new information, even more surprises will come.

Experimentation and big data

Data are flooding in at rates never before seen—doubling every 18 months—as a result of greater access to customer data from public, proprietary, and purchased sources, as well as new information gathered from Web communities and newly deployed smart assets. These trends are broadly known as "big data." Technology for capturing and analyzing information is widely available at ever-lower price points. But many companies are taking data use to new levels, using IT to support rigorous, constant business experimentation that guides decisions and to test new products, business models, and innovations in customer experience. In some cases, the new approaches help companies make decisions in real time. This trend has the potential to drive a radical transformation in research, innovation, and marketing.

Commentary
Hal Varian | Chief economist, Google

Back in the 1980s, people talked about continuous improvement for process efficiency in manufacturing. Now continuous improvement has moved to a new level: you can take real-time data flows coming into a company and automate decisions based on them. Raw information isn't terribly useful, of course. You need to convert it into information that's searchable, accessible, and manipulable. Most important, you want to convert that information into knowledge you can use to make decisions. The companies that do so are going to have a real edge.

One way to use the data is to run controlled experiments—on how to optimize advertising expenditures, for example. Companies have always tried to experiment, but historically that's been costly. With the computer infrastructure now available, companies can experiment much more easily than they could have in the past. At Google, for instance, we run experiments to figure out improvements in how we manage information. We're also using data to gain insight into how we want to launch redesigns and deploy new capabilities and products.

There will still be a role for gut instinct, but the important thing is to look at problems where quantitative data analysis is possible—like the right color for an ad background—and get them off management's table. Managers can simply ask the statisticians to run an experiment and find out. That frees managers up to focus on the more imponderable questions.

Web-based companies such as Amazon.com, eBay, and Google have been early leaders, testing factors that drive performance—from where to place buttons on a Web page to the sequence of content displayed—to determine what will increase sales and user engagement. The online grocer FreshDirect adjusts prices and promotions daily (sometimes even more frequently) based on data feeds from online transactions, visits by consumers to its Web site, and customer service interactions. Other companies are mining data from social networks in real time. Ford Motor

Company, PepsiCo, and Southwest Airlines, for instance, analyze consumer postings about them on social-media sites such as Facebook and Twitter to gauge the immediate impact of their marketing campaigns and to understand how consumer sentiment about their brands is changing.

Using experimentation and big data as essential components of management decision making requires new capabilities, as well as organizational and cultural change. Most companies are far from accessing all the available data. Some haven't even mastered the technologies needed to capture and analyze the valuable information they *can* access. More commonly, they don't have the right talent and processes to design experiments and extract business value from big data, which require changes in the way many executives now make decisions: trusting instincts and experience over experimentation and rigorous analysis. To get managers at all echelons to accept the value of experimentation, senior leaders must buy into a "test and learn" mind-set and then serve as role models for their teams.

Wiring for a sustainable world

Information technology is both a significant source of environmental emissions and a key enabler of many strategies to mitigate environmental damage. At present, IT's share of the world's environmental footprint is growing because of the ever-increasing demand for IT capacity and services. Electricity produced to power the world's data centers generates greenhouse gases on the scale of countries such as Argentina or the Netherlands, and these emissions could increase fourfold by 2020. McKinsey research has shown, however, that the use of IT in areas such as smart power grids, efficient buildings, and better logistics planning could eliminate five times the carbon emissions that the IT industry produces.

Companies are now taking the first steps to reduce the environmental impact of their IT. For instance, businesses are adopting "green data center" technologies to reduce sharply the energy demand of the ever-multiplying numbers of servers needed to cope with data generated by trends such as distributed cocreation and the Internet of Things (described earlier in this article). Such technologies include virtualization software (which enables the more efficient allocation of software across servers) to decrease the number of servers needed for operations, the cooling of data centers with ambient air to cut energy consumption, and inexpensive, renewable hydroelectric power (which, of course, requires locating data centers in places where it is available). Meanwhile, IT manufacturers are organizing programs to collect and recycle hazardous electronics, diverting them from the waste stream.

IT's bigger role, however, lies in its ability to reduce environmental stress from broader corporate and economic activities. Powerful analytic software that improves logistics and routing for planes, trains, and trucks is already reducing the transportation industry's environmental footprint. In another significant push, utilities around the world are deploying smart meters that can help customers shift electricity usage away from peak periods and thereby reduce the amount of power generated by inefficient and costly peak-load facilities. Smart grids can also improve the efficiency of the transmission and distribution of energy and, when coupled with energy storage facilities, could store electricity generated by renewable-energy technologies, such as solar and wind.

Commentary
Rob Bernard | Chief environmental strategist, Microsoft

When faced with seemingly intractable environmental problems, we often focus on technologies of the future. I would argue, however, that we can realize significant benefits by using *current* technologies more fully. For example, although a mere 10 to 15 percent of our homes and buildings are currently wired with smart meters, we don't need to wait for more widespread usage to achieve major benefits. The Internet and other IT infrastructure we currently have in place and at scale could help us gain insight into our energy consumption behavior that would enable us to reduce, by more than 30 percent, the energy our buildings consume. Our phones are another latent source of insight: they carry our schedules and can track our location by using GPS technology. What if we used this information to let our buildings "know" when they are empty? Similarly, the tech industry has been remarkably successful at linking disconnected pieces of information across data networks, via online collaboration tools or through Web services like Facebook. What if the social-networking technology behind Facebook was applied to our commutes? This could enable people who live nearby and who are in our trusted networks to share transportation. Sustainability, in short, could be the next killer app—but not without substantial changes in human behavior. Technology alone is not enough.

Imagining anything as a service

Technology now enables companies to monitor, measure, customize, and bill for asset use at a much more fine-grained level than ever before. Asset owners can therefore create services around what have traditionally been sold as products. Business-to-business (B2B) customers like these service offerings because they allow companies to purchase units of a service and to account for them as a variable cost rather than undertake large capital investments. Consumers also like this "paying only for what you use" model, which helps them avoid large expenditures, as well as the hassles of buying and maintaining a product.

For years, jet engine manufacturers have been delivering units of thrust as a service—"power by the hour," as some in the industry call it. Now, the growth of "cloud computing" (accessing computer resources provided through networks rather than running software or storing data on a local computer) represents a similar shift in the IT industry. Consumer acceptance of Web-based cloud services for everything from e-mail to video is of course becoming universal, and companies are following suit. Software as a service (SaaS), which enables organizations to access services such as customer relationship management, is growing at a 17 percent annual rate. The biotechnology company Genentech, for example, uses Google Apps for e-mail and to create documents and spreadsheets, bypassing capital investments in servers and software licenses. This development has created a wave of computing capabilities delivered as a service, including infrastructure, platforms, applications, and content.

Innovating in services, where the end user is an integral part of the system, requires a mind-set fundamentally different from the one involved in designing products.

Business leaders should be alert to opportunities for transforming product offerings into services, because their competitors will undoubtedly be exploring these avenues. In this disruptive view of assets, physical and intellectual capital combine to create platforms for a new array of service offerings. But innovating in services, where the end user is an integral part of the system, requires a mind-set fundamentally different from the one involved in designing products.

The age of the multisided business model

Multisided business models create value through interactions among multiple players rather than traditional one-on-one transactions or information exchanges. In the media industry, advertising is a classic example of how these models work. Newspapers, magazines, and television stations offer content to their audiences while generating a significant portion of their revenues from third parties: advertisers. Other revenue, often through subscriptions, comes directly from consumers. More recently, this advertising-supported model has proliferated on the Internet, underwriting Web content sites, as well as services such as search and e-mail (see trend number seven, "Imagining anything as a service"). It is now spreading to new markets, such as enterprise software: Spiceworks offers IT-management applications to 950,000 users at no cost, while it collects advertising from B2B companies that want access to IT professionals.

Technology is propagating new, equally powerful forms of multisided business models. In some information businesses, for example, data gathered from one set of users generate revenue when the business charges a separate set of customers for information services based on that data. Take Sermo, an online community of physicians who join (free of charge) to pose questions to other members, participate in discussion groups, and read medical articles. Third parties such as pharmaceutical companies, health care organizations, financial institutions, and government bodies pay for access to the anonymous interactions and polls of Sermo's members.

As more people migrate to online activities, network effects can magnify the value of multisided business models. The "freemium" model is a case in point: a group of customers enjoy free services supported by those who pay a premium for special use. Flickr (online storage of photos), Pandora (online music), and Skype (online communication) not only use this kind of cross-subsidization but also demonstrate the leveraging effect of networks—the greater the number of free users, the more valuable the service becomes for all customers. Pandora harnesses the massive amounts of data from its free users to refine its music recommendations. All Flickr users benefit from a larger photo-posting community, all Skype members from an expanded universe of people with whom to connect.

Other companies find that when their core business is part of a network, valuable data (sometimes called "exhaust data") are generated as a by-product. MasterCard, for instance, has built an advisory unit based on data the company gathers from its core credit card business: it analyzes consumer purchasing patterns and sells aggregated findings to merchants and others that want a better reading on buying trends. CHEP, a logistics-services provider, captures data on a significant portion of the transportation volume of the fastest-moving consumer goods and is now building a transportation-management business to take advantage of this visibility.

Not all companies, of course, could benefit from multisided models. But for those that can, a good starting point for testing them is to take inventory of all the data in a company's businesses (including data flowing from customer interactions) and then ask, "Who might find this information valuable?" Another provocative thought: "What would happen if we provided our product or service free of charge?" or—more important, perhaps—"What if a competitor did so?" The responses should provide indications of the opportunities for disruption, as well as of vulnerabilities.

Shoshana Zuboff explains how new business models could change the nature of capitalism, on page 44.

Innovating from the bottom of the pyramid

Disruptive business models arise when technology combines with extreme market conditions, such as customer demand for very low price points, poor infrastructure, hard-to-access suppliers, and low cost curves for talent. In parts of rural Africa, for instance, traditional retail-banking models have difficulty taking root. Consumers have low incomes and often lack the standard documentation (such as ID cards or even addresses) required to open bank accounts. But Safaricom, a telecom provider, offers banking services to eight million Africans through its M-PESA mobile-phone service (*M* stands for "mobile," *pesa* is Swahili for "money"). The company also allows a network of shops and gas stations that sell telecommunications airtime to load virtual cash onto cell phones.

In China, another technology-based model brings order to the vast, highly dispersed strata of smaller manufacturing facilities. Many small businesses around the world have difficulty finding Chinese manufacturers to meet specific needs. Some of these manufacturers are located in remote areas, and their capabilities can vary widely. Alibaba, China's leading B2B exchange, with more than 30 million members, helps members share data on their manufacturing services with potential customers and handles online payments and other transactions. Its network, in effect, offers Chinese manufacturing capacity as a service, enabling small businesses anywhere in the world to identify suppliers quickly and scale up rapidly to meet demand.

Hundreds of companies are now appearing on the global scene from emerging markets, with offerings ranging from a low-cost bespoke tutoring service to the remote monitoring of sophisticated air-conditioning systems around the world. For most global incumbents, these represent a new *type* of competitor: they are not only challenging the dominant players' growth plans in developing markets but also exporting their extreme models to developed ones. To respond, global players must plug into the local networks of entrepreneurs, fast-growing businesses, suppliers, investors, and influencers spawning such disruptions. Some global companies, such as GE, are locating research centers in these cauldrons of creativity to spur their own innovations there. Others, such as Philips and SAP, are now investing in local companies to nurture new, innovative products for export that complement their core businesses.

Commentary
Rob Salkowitz | Author of *Young World Rising: How Youth, Technology, and Entrepreneurship Are Changing the World from the Bottom Up*

A critical feature of innovation in emerging markets is the speed with which large concentrations of young people embrace technology. In my work, I've seen everything from young entrepreneurs in Ghana who use simple cell phone–based text messaging to combat pharmaceutical counterfeiting, to entrepreneurs in India who develop mobile apps to provide local producers with better visibility into market conditions.

These youthful, indigenous innovators use their deep knowledge of local customers to take advantage of the low cost, simplicity, and accessibility of new technologies, and they are building new business models around resource-constrained conditions. One African software developer coined the term "tropical tolerance" to describe robust product features that compensate for gaps in infrastructure, workplace skills, and government transparency.

As data networks and mobile devices hit critical mass in countries such as Brazil, India, Mexico, South Africa, and Vietnam, new business models and new sources of economic opportunity are emerging. Multinational businesses can learn much from the skills demonstrated by the current crop of young-world innovators. To succeed locally, established players need to adopt lightweight strategies that are scaled for local needs and to offer products priced in small units of local currency. In doing so, they will also pave the way for big improvements in the lives of the next billion or two billion global customers.

Producing public good on the grid

In the years ahead, technology will facilitate the creation of new types of public goods while helping to manage them more effectively. Take the challenges of rising urbanization. About half of the world's people now live in urban areas, and that share is projected to rise to 70 percent by 2050. Creative public policies that incorporate new technologies could help ease the economic and social strains of population density. "Wired" cities might be one approach. London, Singapore, and Stockholm have used smart assets to manage traffic congestion in their urban cores, and many cities throughout the world are deploying these technologies to improve the reliability and predictability of mass-transit systems. Similarly, networked smart water grids will be critical to address the need for clean water.

Technology can also improve the delivery and effectiveness of many public services. Law-enforcement agencies are using smart assets—video cameras and data analytics—to create maps that define high-crime zones and direct additional police resources to them. Cloud computing and collaboration technologies can improve educational services, giving young and adult students alike access to low-cost content, online instructors, and communities of fellow learners. Public policy also stands to become more transparent and effective thanks to a number of new open-data initiatives. At the UK Web site FixMyStreet.com, for example, citizens report, view, and discuss local problems, such as graffiti and the illegal dumping of waste, and interact with local officials who provide updates on actions to solve them.

Exploiting technology's full potential in the public sphere means reimagining the way public goods are created, delivered, and managed. Setting out a bold vision for what a wired, smart community could accomplish is a starting point for setting strategy. Putting that vision in place requires forward-thinking yet prudent leadership that sets milestones, adopts flexible test-and-learn methods, and measures success. Inertia hobbles many public organizations, so leaders must craft incentives tailored to public projects and embrace novel, unfamiliar collaborations among governments, technology providers, other businesses, nongovernmental organizations, and citizens.

•   •   •

The pace of technology and business change will only accelerate, and the impact of the trends above will broaden and deepen. For some organizations, they will unlock significant competitive advantages; for others, dealing with the disruption they bring will be a major challenge. Our broad message is that organizations should incorporate an understanding of the trends into their strategic thinking to help identify new market opportunities, invent new ways of doing business, and compete with an ever-growing number of innovative rivals. ○

The authors wish to acknowledge the important contributions of their colleague Angela Hung Byers.

Jacques Bughin is a director in McKinsey's Brussels office; **Michael Chui** is a senior fellow of the McKinsey Global Institute; **James Manyika** is a director in the San Francisco office and a director of the McKinsey Global Institute.

Listen to additional expert commentary on these technology trends via podcast on mckinseyquarterly.com.

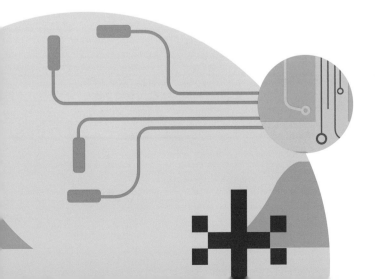

Further reading on the ten tech-enabled business trends

1. Distributed cocreation moves into the mainstream

Jacques Bughin, Michael Chui, and Brad Johnson, "The next step in open innovation," mckinseyquarterly.com, June 2008.

Michael Chui, Andy Miller, and Roger P. Roberts, "Six ways to make Web 2.0 work," mckinseyquarterly .com, February 2009.

Clay Shirky, *Here Comes Everybody: The Power of Organizing Without Organizations*, reprint edition, New York, NY: Penguin, 2009.

2. Making the network the organization

Lowell L. Bryan and Claudia I. Joyce, *Mobilizing Minds: Creating Wealth from Talent in the 21st-Century Organization*, New York, NY: McGraw-Hill, 2007.

Albert-Laszlo Barabasi, *Linked: How Everything is Connected to Everything Else and What It Means for Business, Science, and Everyday Life*, New York, NY: Plume, 2009.

3. Collaboration at scale

Andrew McAfee, *Enterprise 2.0: New Collaborative Tools for Your Organization's Toughest Challenges*, first edition, Cambridge, MA: Harvard Business School Press, 2009.

Erik Brynjolfsson and Adam Saunders, *Wired for Innovation: How Information Technology is Reshaping the Economy*, Cambridge, MA: The MIT Press, 2009.

James Manyika, Kara Sprague, and Lareina Yee, "Using technology to improve workforce collaboration," whatmatters.mckinseydigital.com, October 27, 2009.

Wolf Richter, David Bray, and William Dutton, "Cultivating the value of networked individuals," in Jonathan Foster, *Collaborative Information Behavior: User Engagement and Communication Sharing*, Hershey, PA: IGI Global, 2010.

4. The growing 'Internet of Things'

Michael Chui, Markus Löffler, and Roger Roberts, "The Internet of Things," mckinseyquarterly.com, March 2010.

Hal R. Varian, "Computer mediated transactions," Ely Lecture to the American Economics Association, Atlanta, GA, January 3, 2010.

Bernhard Boser, Joe Kahn, and Kris Pister, "Smart dust: Wireless networks of millimeter-scale sensor nodes," Electronics Research Laboratory Research Summary, 1999.

5. Experimentation and big data

Stefan Thomke, "Enlightened experimentation: The new imperative for innovation," *Harvard Business Review*, February 2001, Volume 79, Number 2, pp. 66–75.

Thomas H. Davenport, Jeanne G. Harris, and Robert Morison, *Analytics at Work: Smarter Decisions, Better Results*, Cambridge, MA: Harvard Business Press, 2010.

David Bollier, *The Promise and Peril of Big Data*, The Aspen Institute, 2010.

Janaki Akella, Timo Kubach, Markus Löffler, and Uwe Schmid, "Data-driven management: Bringing more science into management," McKinsey Technology Initiative white paper.

"The data deluge," *Economist* special report, February 25, 2010.

6. Wiring for a sustainable world
Giulio Boccaletti, Markus Löffler, and Jeremy M. Oppenheim, "How IT can cut carbon emissions," mckinseyquarterly.com, October 2008.

William Forrest, James M. Kaplan, and Noah Kindler, "Data centers: How to cut carbon emissions *and* costs," mckinseyquarterly.com, November 2008.

7. Imagining anything as a service
Nicholas Carr, *The Big Switch: Rewiring the World, from Edison to Google*, reprint edition, New York, NY: W. W. Norton & Company, 2009.

IBM and University of Cambridge, "Succeeding through service innovation: A service perspective for education, research, business and government," Cambridge Service Science, Management, and Engineering Symposium, Cambridge, July 14–15, 2007.

Peter Mell and Tim Grance, "The NIST definition of cloud computing," *National Institute of Standards and Technology*, Version 15, October 7, 2009.

8. The age of the multisided business model
Chris Anderson, *Free: How Today's Smartest Businesses Profit by Giving Something for Nothing*, New York, NY: Hyperion, 2009.

Annabelle Gawer ed., *Platforms, Markets and Innovation*, Cheltenham, UK: Edward Elgar Publishing, 2010.

9. Innovating from the bottom of the pyramid
Jeffrey R. Immelt, Vijay Govindarajan, and Chris Trimble, "How GE is disrupting itself," *Harvard Business Review*, October 2009, Volume 87, Number 10, pp. 56–65.

C. K. Prahalad, *The Fortune at the Bottom of the Pyramid: Eradicating Poverty Through Profits*, fifth edition, Philadelphia, PA: Wharton School Publishing, July 2009.

10. Producing public good on the grid
Jason Baumgarten and Michael Chui, "E-government 2.0," mckinseyquarterly.com, July 2009.

Bas Boorsma and Wolfgang Wagner, "Connected urban development: Innovation for sustainability," *NATOA Journal*, Winter 2007, Volume 15, Number 4, pp. 5–9.

O'Reilly Radar Government 2.0 (radar.oreilly.com)

Connected Urban Development (connectedurbandevelopment.org)

Building a smarter planet (asmarterplanet.com)

Shoshana Zuboff

Creating value in the age of distributed capitalism

Artwork by Celia Johnson

A historic transition in capitalism
is unfolding as the era of mass
consumption gives way to one built
on individuals and their desires.

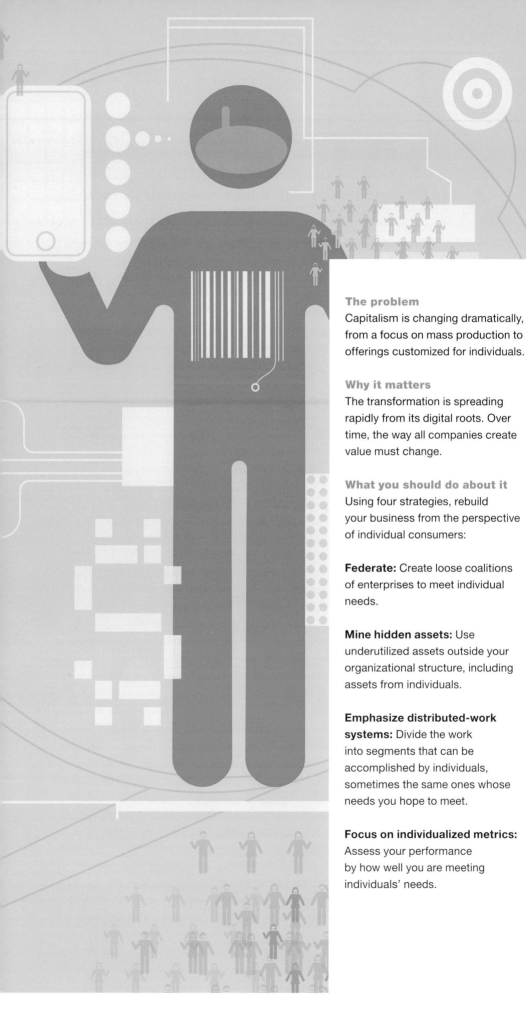

The problem
Capitalism is changing dramatically, from a focus on mass production to offerings customized for individuals.

Why it matters
The transformation is spreading rapidly from its digital roots. Over time, the way all companies create value must change.

What you should do about it
Using four strategies, rebuild your business from the perspective of individual consumers:

Federate: Create loose coalitions of enterprises to meet individual needs.

Mine hidden assets: Use underutilized assets outside your organizational structure, including assets from individuals.

Emphasize distributed-work systems: Divide the work into segments that can be accomplished by individuals, sometimes the same ones whose needs you hope to meet.

Focus on individualized metrics: Assess your performance by how well you are meeting individuals' needs.

Capitalism is a book of many chapters—and we are beginning a new one. Every century or so, fundamental changes in the nature of consumption create new demand patterns that existing enterprises can't meet. When a majority of people want things that remain priced at a premium under the old institutional regime—a condition I call the "premium puzzle"—the ground becomes extremely fertile for wholly new classes of competitors that can fulfill the new demands at an affordable price. A premium puzzle existed in the auto industry before Henry Ford and the Model T and in the music industry before Steve Jobs and the iPod.

The consumption shift in Ford's time was from the elite to the masses; today, we are moving from an era of mass consumption to one focused on the individual. Sharp increases in higher education, standards of living, social complexity, and longevity over the past century gave rise to a new desire for individual self-determination: having control over what matters, having one's voice heard, and having social connections on one's own terms. The leading edge of consumption is now moving from products and services to tools and relationships enabled by interactive technologies. Amazon.com, Apple, eBay, and YouTube are familiar examples of companies solving today's premium puzzle. Lesser-known companies like CellBazaar (in emerging-market mobile commerce), TutorVista (in tutoring), and Livemocha (in language education) also abound.

It would be easy to construe these as isolated cases of innovation and industry change, but I believe they represent much more: a mutation in capitalism itself. What's the difference? Innovations improve the framework in which enterprises produce and deliver goods and services. Mutations create new frameworks; they are not simply new technologies, though they do leverage technologies to do new things. Historically, mutations have superseded innovations when fundamental shifts in what people want require a new approach to enterprise: new purposes, new methods, new outcomes.

In the same way that mass production moved the locus of industry from small shops to huge factories, today's mutations have the potential to shift us away from business models based on economies of scale, asset intensification, concentration, and central control. That's not to say factories are going away; their role in supplying quality, low-cost goods, including the technologies underpinning the shift to more individualized consumption, is secure. Yet even mass production is becoming less homogenous (consider the ability to order custom sneakers from Nike). And for many goods and services, new business frameworks are emerging: federations of enterprises—from a variety of sectors—that share collaborative values and goals are increasingly capable of distributing valued assets directly to individuals, enabling them to determine exactly what they will consume, as well as when and how. This shift not only changes the basis of competition for companies but also blurs—and even removes—the boundaries between entire industries, along with those that have existed between producers and consumers. The music and newspaper industries ignored this shift, to their great detriment. I believe *all* businesses will have to find ways to adapt to this new world if they want to grow.

The economist Joseph Schumpeter cautioned his readers not to expect new forms of economic development to announce themselves with a grand flourish. "The 'new thing,'" he wrote, "need not be Bessemer steel or the explosion motor. It can be the Deerfoot sausage."[1] My hope is that this article will help executives see the links between today's "Deerfoot sausages," recognize the magnitude of the economic transition these mutations portend, and begin setting—or at least contemplating—a new course in this changing world.

It won't be easy. But enterprises that can leverage technology *and* real-world social connections to solve their piece of the premium puzzle—creating individualized ways to consume goods and services at a radically reduced cost—will prosper as they realize wholly new sources of value that remain invisible to companies still bound by conventional business models.

Mutation and distributed capitalism

The last chapter of capitalism unfolded in the early 20th century and was epitomized by Henry Ford and his Model T. At first, the Model T was simply regarded as the affordable car that finally made the Ford Motor Company profitable. But it turned out to be much more. The Model T embodied a mutation we now call mass production. It solved the premium puzzle of its time, reducing the price of an automobile by 60 percent or more, and thrived in the emerging environment of mass consumption.

Ford's Model T not only changed the entire framework of production but also set the stage for another automotive pioneer, Alfred Sloan, to establish the modern, professionally managed, multidivisional company as the basis for wealth creation in the 20th century. In the end, the Model T's power had nothing to do with cars per se. Mass production could be applied to anything—and it was. It provided the gateway to a new era because it revealed a parallel universe of economic value hidden in mass-market consumers and accessible to companies that could create affordable versions of previously unattainable goods such as cars. That potential for wealth creation remained invisible to those who clung to the 19th-century framework of small-factory, proprietary capitalism.

[1] Joseph Schumpeter, "The creative response in economic history," *Journal of Economic History*, 1947, Volume 7, Number 2, pp. 149–59.

The mass-production business model has come under assault during the past decade, perhaps most successfully by the combination of Apple's iPod and its music service, iTunes. The iPod is a cool gadget, but (like the Model T) it is also a gateway product, one of the first to achieve both scale and commercial success while expressing a new mutation. The iPod and iTunes reinvented music consumption by starting with the listener's individual space, which I call "I-space." Apple rescued musical assets from a faltering business model—the compact disc—and bypassed the industry's costly legacy systems and routes to market. It supported users in reconfiguring their music as they saw fit. Apple is the largest music retailer in the United States today. But I would argue that the real breakthrough had nothing to do with music per se. The true source of value, which had been invisible to the music industry, resided in Apple's ability to reinvent the consumption experience from the viewpoint of the individual, at a fraction of the old cost.

The iPod—and its successors, the iPhone and the iPad—are part of the first wave of what I call "distributed capitalism," which encompasses the myriad ways in which production and consumption increasingly depend on distributed assets, distributed information, and distributed social and management systems.[2] Distributed capitalism could not thrive without the technologies associated with the Internet, mobile computing, wireless broadband, and related developments in digitization and software applications. But just using these technologies does not ensure success.

Winning mutations—those that create value by offering consumers individualized goods and services at a radically reduced cost—express a convergence of technological capabilities and the values associated with individual self-determination. The iPod and scores of other successful mutations have infiltrated the economy sufficiently to provide preferred alternatives to established sources of goods and services across many industries. Taken together, they have begun expressing a distinctly new "genetic code" that encompasses five essential functions:

Inversion. The old logic of wealth creation worked from the perspective of the organization and its requirements—for efficiency, cost reductions, revenues, growth, earnings per share (EPS), and returns on investment (ROI)—and pointed inward. The new logic starts with the individual end user. Instead of "What do we have and how can we sell it to you?" good business practices start by asking "Who are you?" "What do you need?" and "How can we help?" This inverted thinking makes it possible to identify the assets that represent real value for each individual. Cash flow and profitability are derived from those assets.

---

[2] Distributed capitalism—and the shift away from business models based on economies of scale, asset intensification, concentration, and central control—was first described in my 2002 book, *The Support Economy: Why Corporations Are Failing Individuals and the Next Episode of Capitalism*, which I wrote with Jim Maxmin.

Rescue. Once valuable assets have been identified, they must be rescued from old, costly industry structures. Assets—such as knowledge, music, books, medical diagnoses and treatments, teaching, information, skills, and people—have been concentrated inside organizations, where they can be managed and controlled to fulfill corporate goals, procedures, and targets. Rescuing assets means digitizing them whenever possible for easy and affordable distribution to users in I-space.

Bypass. Many current mutations have arisen outside the domain of existing institutions, and often in spite of their determined resistance. By leveraging digital technologies and new social arrangements, these mutations are bypassing existing institutional structures—human, physical, organizational, technological, or financial—and connecting individuals directly to the assets they seek. Just as a coronary bypass ignores a damaged blood vessel and takes blood to its destination another way, so mutations like iTunes or distance learning simply bypass the unnecessary costs, outdated assumptions, and value-destroying practices of legacy systems.

Reconfiguration. Once individuals have the assets they want, they must be able to reconfigure those assets according to their own values, interests, convenience, and pleasure. A teenager, for instance, may use her iPod Touch and an application called Pandora to assemble an entire personalized "radio station" while at the same time learning Mandarin Chinese at the kitchen table on Sunday afternoon through an online classroom based thousands of miles from her home.

Support. Successful mutations offer consumers the digital tools, platforms, and social relationships that support them in living their lives as they choose. The new sources of economic value can be discovered and realized in I-space only when consumption strengthens the sense of personal control, delivers opportunities for voicing ideas, and enables freely chosen social connections. The emerging logic of distributed capitalism rewards enterprises that realign their practices with the interests of the end consumer and punishes enterprises that try to impose their own internal requirements or, worse yet, maximize their own benefit at the expense of the individual end user.

Sometimes mutations can stumble and betray their genetic inheritance, as in Facebook's missteps regarding user privacy. But what's important is that all these early mutations address individual needs that are invisible from the perspective of a typical company and target the kinds of trapped assets that are both valuable to individuals *and* easily digitized.

The next test for distributed capitalism

Can distributed capitalism go further? What happens when it confronts forms of physical assets and social support that cannot be reduced to information—arenas where face-to-face experience is essential? This is when distributed capitalism, which until now has manifested itself almost entirely in the digital world, will begin to mature as it takes aim at core economic functions with a second wave of more complex mutations that combine virtual and real-world assets.

Early mutations in health care

The premium puzzle has become the defining characteristic of most individuals' health care experiences: the health care one can afford is rarely the health care one wants. This problem has been felt most acutely in the United States, where expenditures on health care have grown faster than GDP for three decades, while quality and performance have declined. But it is sure to intensify elsewhere as aging populations make it harder for governments to finance today's systems.

In the vacuum created by these frustrations, many people concluded that they must first try to help themselves and their families before turning to professionals. Mutations such as WebMD arose, aimed at capturing, interpreting, and distributing information once held closely within the medical enclave. Such sites are now credible ways to access information that doctors just won't provide at a price people can afford—and sometimes at any price.

Another group of mutations has emerged in the areas of home-based diagnosis, monitoring, and testing. Each mutation is designed, in its own way, to invert the process of information gathering, rescue critical diagnostic capabilities from professional enclaves, connect those assets directly to the individuals who want them, enable users to configure them as they wish, and support their use with timely feedback. There are tests for everything from blood pressure to marijuana use to HIV infection. Distribution has even gone mobile, with cell phones that monitor blood glucose levels and heart rates, connect you to hot lines, signal the calorie count of your cheeseburger, or register the energy you burn as you walk your dog.

Radical mutation in elder care: A case study

One of the most intractable premium puzzles in the health care system today is elder care. The average annual cost of nursing-home care in the United States approaches $80,000. Only a small percentage of US residents can afford these prices, while state and federal funding is shrinking. Further, nursing homes tend to be for-profit businesses in which cost imperatives lead to understaffing and low wages. Dismal data on bedsores, medical errors, and elder abuse suggest that elder care as generally practiced is a euphemism for human warehousing on the cheap.

A Maine-based start-up called Elder Power (EP) has taken direct aim at the elder care premium puzzle. It showcases new capabilities and strategies that integrate digital and face-to-face support, and its initial success provides important guidance on solving today's premium puzzle in the physical world. EP has broken through the economic barriers of elder care. The average monthly cost in Maine exceeds that in the United States as a whole for nursing-home care ($7,000 in Maine versus $6,500 in the rest of the United States); for assisted living ($4,000 versus $3,100); and for 24-hour home care ($24,000 versus $16,200). In contrast, EP has enabled seniors to remain at home at an average monthly cost of $702—$378 for technology and $324 for personalized support. EP enables seniors to be secure, socially enriched, and personally empowered for 3 percent of the average cost of conventional home care in Maine, 10 percent of the average cost of a nursing home, and 18 percent of the average cost of assisted living.

Before explaining how this is possible, I want to offer two caveats. First, the reason I have such detailed information about EP is that my husband and collaborator, Jim Maxmin, is one of its architects. Jim holds shares in the company, which is a for-profit community network whose profits are entirely reinvested in the network to support its neediest participants. Second, EP is a tiny experiment, with (as of March 2010) 56 members. This group does not, however, represent an easy-to-serve population: many have mild to severe Alzheimer's disease.

EP has a significant technology component. Each elder person's home is equipped with a "digital spine," with members opting for various technology levels, from the basic tools (emergency alert, a stationary webcam, a videophone, and a computer interface) to more elaborate systems that include multiple webcams, sensors, and around-the-clock monitoring. A Web site provides access to a community calendar, local services, a story and poetry corner, video clips, advice, e-mail, and an EP Facebook page. There is also a Web-based Elder Power TV network, which features local events such as plays and church services. The technology reassures families that the elder person is well and the network is there to help.

As is crucial to second-wave mutations, the EP model extends beyond the digital realm. EP is a social network that includes members; their families, friends, and neighbors; volunteers; paid staff; and professionals. Each member has a personal advocate within the network who helps coordinate the use of EP's services. In addition, EP expects members to take an active role in their own well-being and to help others in the network. A partially disabled housebound member, for example, oversees the daily monitoring.

Financial surpluses generated by the EP model help to offset the expenses of volunteers and to reward them with meal vouchers, gasoline, film tickets, and the like. This combination of paid and unpaid support services means that one registered nurse employed by EP can serve more than 60 remote seniors. EP estimates it would take 40 to 50 volunteers to support 1,000 seniors.

Strategies for radical mutation

Elder Power exemplifies four new strategies for pulling off radical mutations in arenas where real-world—not just digital—assets are integral to the individual experience. First, it's a federation, by which I mean a branded constellation of enterprises drawn from many industry sectors that revolves around the individual—such as a local utility that gives EP members top priority in the monitoring and emergency maintenance of home electrical and heating systems. Second, EP identifies, uses, and remunerates underutilized community and network resources (services, spaces, people, capabilities, and goods) that are "hidden in plain sight," such as the local high-school cafeteria, where elders dine weekly after the regular lunch period ends, or an extra bedroom in a member's home that can be used for another elder to recuperate after a hospital stay.

Third, EP leverages available resources by distributing work: one volunteer or member might make two daily phone calls. Another might transport a group of seniors to lunch once a week. A third might coordinate the evening meal for three seniors in her neighborhood. Finally, EP relies on what I call "I-metrics," which realign business practices with the experience, values, and priorities of the people an enterprise serves. For EP, I-metrics reflect subjective evaluations such as "I feel safe and happy at home," "I feel needed," or "I can get down to the back meadow to see the spring flowers."

Elder Power is far from the only place where the importance (and sometimes the difficulty) of implementing these strategies is revealing itself. Consider federation: since Apple understood that its iPod users wanted to be connected to one another, it didn't say, "Go buy a cell phone, because connection isn't our business." Instead, it broadened the scope of its offerings, creating new partnerships and business models at each turn as the stand-alone iPod morphed into the iPhone. The choice to host applications on the iPhone further accelerated this process, reimagining the iPhone as a portal to an ever-widening "protofederation" of support providers.

But creating effective federations is challenging. Apple, like Facebook, has struggled to define its relationship with application developers. Both companies began by regarding applications as simply hosted transactions— a manifestation of the old genome—but are evolving toward a recognition that applications are a seamless extension of their end users' experience. And both are confronting the following challenge: how much control will they, as the coordinators of their respective federations, exercise, compared with other member enterprises and with end users?

Amazon.com has exerted control by requiring companies that participate in its marketplace to comply with its customer standards and be subject to its methods of "engineered trust," such as published customer evaluations. These kinds of relationships are the early building blocks of federated support networks.

Embracing distributed capitalism

While Elder Power is operating on a tiny scale, its way of solving the premium puzzle in elder care offers a vivid demonstration of what I believe will be core features of the 21st-century economy: creating new social and enterprise frameworks that operate on behalf of individual end users, enabling them with the tools, platforms, and relationships to live their lives as they choose. The range of individual support underlying many of today's mutations is wide (exhibit).

What should executives do to ensure that their organizations will grow in this new world? For starters, it's critical to question the old logic and vocabulary of competitive strategy. For example, one executive asked me

A new wave of business mutation is bringing personalization and tailored support to the core of the economy.

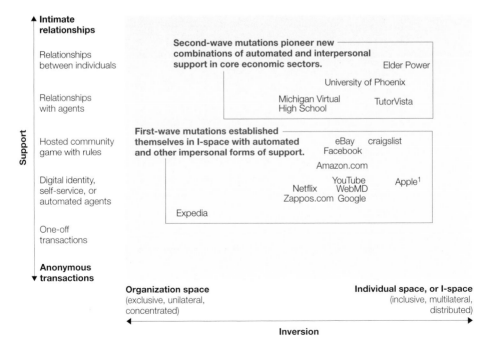

[1] Specifically, iPod, iPhone, iPad, and applications.

Source: Shoshana Zuboff

One way for executives to shake up their strategic thinking is to start with the radical question of how a mutation could destroy the boundaries of their industries.

recently, "How do I play out what a mutation might look like in my industry?" But in fact, mutations do not arise within industries; they arise as reconfigurations of assets defined by the unmet needs of individual end users. Mutations take root in individual space, and they quickly blur the boundaries of industries, sectors, and enterprises—ultimately making those boundaries obsolete. Is Amazon.com, for instance, in the retail, the logistics, or the Web-services industry? The question no longer makes sense.

As mutations move into the physical world, it's easy to imagine a similar blurring of boundaries: road construction might become part of transportation or sustainability solutions; airlines might be core elements of leisure, logistics, or environmental solutions; banks could become part of wellbeing, education, or active-aging solutions. In short, mutations that upend industries can come from anywhere, and conventional forms of market analysis and competitive strategy will miss those mutations.

One way for executives to shake up their strategic thinking is to start with the radical question of how a mutation could destroy the boundaries of their industries. In my mind, that danger increases under the following circumstances:

1. The products or services you offer are affordable to few but desired by many.

2. Trust between you and your customer has fractured. The average person's trust in business has been in steep decline for the past 30 years, and the distance between what today's businesses can deliver and what individuals want is only growing. This problem makes all consumer-facing industries—especially financial services, health care, insurance, autos, airlines, utilities, media, education, and pharmaceuticals—particularly vulnerable.

3. Your business model is concentrated, with a high level of fixed costs, a large percentage of which could be distributed, delegated to collaborators, or shifted to the virtual world. Here, too, most existing industries are deeply vulnerable.

4. Your organizational structures, systems, and activities can be replaced by flexible, responsive, low-cost networks. A neighborhood watch, citizen journalists, online peer support, and peer-to-peer reviews and information sharing are all examples.

5. There are hidden assets, outside institutional boundaries, that are underutilized but could replace your fixed costs, add capacity, or add new capabilities.

6. You don't have all the tangible or intangible assets required to meet your customers' needs.

7. Your end users have needs and desires that you haven't imagined and have no way to learn about. Unless you make a strategic commitment to explore I-space, you'll learn about this vulnerability only when your end users migrate elsewhere. This has already been the experience of executives in industries such as recorded music, newspapers, broadcast news, and travel.

●   ●   ●

Despite the drama and significance of historic transitions in capitalism, they do not announce themselves. The pattern of change is one of overlapping and interwoven fields of transition rather than clean, unidirectional breaks. For those of us living through these transitions, they can be confusing and frustrating; resources invested in innovation serve only to fix what was, bringing us no closer to the future. But these times are also rich with unique opportunities for companies able to decipher the emerging pattern of mutation and to convert that understanding into new business models that support the complex needs of the 21st-century individual. ○

Shoshana Zuboff, the former Charles Edward Wilson Professor of Business Administration at the Harvard Business School, is the author of *In the Age of the Smart Machine: The Future of Work and Power* (Basic Books, 1989), among other books.

The $2.6 trillion opportunity

Norbert Dörr, Acha Leke, and Arend van Wamelen

Africa's economies are on the move. The continent's GDP rose by
4.9 percent a year from 2000 through 2008, more than twice its pace in
the 1980s and '90s. Africa's collective GDP reached $1.6 trillion in
2008—roughly equal to Brazil's or Russia's. What's more, Africa was one
of just two economic regions (the other was Asia) where GDP rose
during the global recession of 2009. And new research by the McKinsey
Global Institute (MGI) suggests that by 2020, Africa's consumer-
facing, agricultural, natural-resource, and infrastructure sectors will
collectively represent $2.6 trillion in annual revenue opportunities
for domestic and foreign companies.

Underpinning the continent's recent growth surge: greater stability and
economic reform. To start, several African countries halted their deadly
hostilities, creating the political stability necessary to foster growth. Next,
many of Africa's governments lowered inflation, trimmed foreign debt,
and shrunk their budget deficits. Finally, many African regimes increasingly adopted beneficial policies, such as privatizing state-owned
enterprises, reducing trade barriers, and bolstering regulatory systems.
These structural changes not only enabled a stronger private business
sector to emerge but are also fueling an African productivity revolution.
After declining through the 1980s and 1990s, labor productivity started
rising in 2000 and has climbed by a stout 2.7 percent a year since then.
Companies are achieving greater economies of scale, increasing their
investments, and becoming more competitive.

Africa also is gaining access to unprecedented levels of international
capital. Foreign direct investment increased from $9 billion in 2000 to a
whopping $62 billion in 2008—relative to GDP, almost as large as the
flow into China. Returns on foreign direct investment in Africa surpass

Also in this report:

Establishing priorities in Africa

+

How we do it: Three executives
offer advice on competing in Africa

Painted by Katongo

Tinga Tinga art from
Tanzania
Tingatingastudio.com

those in any other region of the world, according to data by the United
Nations Conference on Trade and Development (UNCTAD).[1] This surge—
and Africa's growth more broadly—therefore aren't just a result of
the past decade's global commodities boom. The continent does boast a
bounty of oil, minerals, and other natural resources, yet they directly
accounted for barely one-quarter of Africa's GDP growth from 2000
through 2008. The rest came from other sectors, including wholesale
and retail trade, transportation, manufacturing, and telecommunications
(which, along with banking, tourism, textiles, and construction, also
contributed significantly to the growth in foreign direct investment).

While many of Africa's 50-plus countries face thorny challenges—among
them poverty and disease—and could yet suffer economic setbacks, a
confluence of powerful social, demographic, and economic trends suggests
that the continent's long-term growth is sustainable and may even
accelerate. In 1980, for example, just 28 percent of Africans lived in cities.
Today, 40 percent do, a proportion comparable to China's and surpass-
ing India's. As more Africans move to urban jobs, their incomes are rising.
In 2008, roughly 85 million African households earned at least $5,000—
the level above which people in emerging markets start spending roughly
half their income on items other than food. The number of households
with discretionary income is projected to rise by 50 percent over the next
decade, reaching 128 million.

In short, it's time for senior executives to stop asking "Why Africa?"
and to start asking "Why aren't we doing more there?" The four industry
groups described on the following pages convey the magnitude of the
opportunity at stake.

[1] See also Paul Collier, "The case for investing in Africa," mckinseyquarterly.com, June 2010.

The full report, *Lions on the move: The progress and
potential of African economies*, is available free of charge
on mckinsey.com/mgi.

The rise of Africa's urban consumer

Africa is already one of the world's fastest-growing consumer markets, expanding two to three times faster than those in Organisation for Economic Co-operation and Development (OECD) countries. And African households spent $860 billion in 2008, more than households in India or Russia. Rising incomes will propel spending further. Indeed, if the continent's combined GDP continues to grow by 5 percent a year, African households will spend $1.4 trillion in 2020.

Spending patterns will shift as more households gain discretionary spending power. Food and beverage consumption should increase the most in absolute terms, as consumers buy greater quantities and higher-quality items. Household spending will grow more rapidly, however, in categories such as retail banking, telecommunications, education, housing, and health care.

Urban markets will be particularly attractive to global companies. By 2020, the five largest markets—Cairo, Johannesburg, Cape Town, Lagos, and Alexandria—will each boast consumer spending of $25 billion or more, comparable to Mumbai's and New Delhi's. Successful consumer-facing companies will tailor their products and strategies for Africa. Clearly, they need to devise new strategies for serving low-income consumers. And companies also must find ways to overcome the challenge of poor infrastructure and formal retailing's low penetration (which could be counteracted, for example, by selling not only through formal stores but also through street vendors and other informal channels).

	Household spending, 2008,[1] $ billion	Household spending growth, 2008–20,[1] $ billion	Compound annual growth rate (CAGR), 2008–20,[1] %
Food and beverage	369	175	3.3
Housing	144	101	4.5
Nonfood consumer goods	97	62	4.2
Health care	51	32	4.2
Telecom	46	35	4.9
Banking	28	30	6.2
Education	26	21	4.9
Other	101	60	4.0
Total	**861**	**515**	**4.0**

[1] Figures do not sum to total, because of rounding.

Source: Euromonitor; *World Development Indicators*, World Bank; McKinsey Global Institute analysis

Seeding a green revolution

Africa has enormous potential to raise the volume and value of its agricultural production and to expand related business activities. Although this is a daunting challenge, MGI estimates that the value of the continent's annual agricultural output could be increased from $280 billion today to around $500 billion by 2020 and to $880 billion by 2030. Growth of this magnitude would require meeting three goals: bringing more land into large-scale cultivation, raising yields on key crops to 80 percent of the world average, and shifting 20 percent of cultivation from lower-value crops to higher-value fruits, vegetables, and biofuels.

These goals are challenging but, over a 20-year horizon, also attainable. If Africa meets them, the value of the continent's agricultural production will grow by almost 6 percent annually over the next two decades—twice as fast as it did over the past one. Nearly three-quarters of the absolute increase in output would occur in 11 countries: Angola, Cameroon, Côte d'Ivoire, Ethiopia, Ghana, Kenya, Madagascar, Mozambique, Nigeria, Sudan, and Tanzania.

A "green revolution" in agriculture on this scale would in turn fuel widespread growth among related businesses. Our analysis suggests that upstream input markets would increase from around $8 billion today to $35 billion by 2030. Downstream markets could grow sixfold, reaching $240 billion by 2030. The processing of biofuels is the fastest growing of these opportunities and has the highest margins. Ethanol production could be particularly attractive for Africa's inland oil-importing countries, where high transportation costs raise fuel prices for consumers. Africa also could become a major supplier of biofuels to Europe.

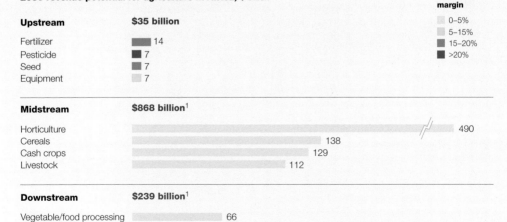

2030 revenue potential for agriculture in Africa, $ billion

Operating margin

- 0–5%
- 5–15%
- 15–20%
- >20%

Upstream	$35 billion
Fertilizer	14
Pesticide	7
Seed	7
Equipment	7

Midstream	$868 billion[1]
Horticulture	490
Cereals	138
Cash crops	129
Livestock	112

Downstream	$239 billion[1]
Vegetable/food processing	66
Grain processing	58
Livestock processing	33
Biofuels processing	23
Other processing	60

[1] Figures do not sum to total, because of rounding.

Source: McKinsey Global Institute analysis

Resources: From strong to stronger

The growth prospects for Africa's resource sectors remain promising. The total value of annual production, we estimate, could increase from $430 billion in 2008 to $540 billion by 2020. Global demand is likely to remain strong for oil, gas, and coal, which together account for roughly 85 percent of Africa's resource production. McKinsey's base-case projections indicate that the continent's production of these commodities, measured by volume, will grow about 2 to 4 percent a year through 2020. The value of oil and gas production will grow the most, by $65 billion and $25 billion, respectively. Iron ore and coal will grow more than any other minerals in terms of value—iron ore by $10 billion, coal by $6 billion.

Meanwhile, the nature of resource deals in Africa is changing and the field of buyers getting more crowded, reflecting the significant influence of China and other new players in the market. To compete for access to resources, companies must increasingly go beyond extraction and provide wider economic benefits, appeal to multiple stakeholders, and deliver benefits quickly. Notably, 23 percent of Africa's resource deals over the past four years were accompanied by commitments to invest in infrastructure and related industries, compared with just 1 percent in the 1990s. Political risk remains a key consideration for both foreign and regional companies looking to expand in Africa, given the large and long-term nature of resource investments. Diversifying operations across countries will remain an important means of managing risk.

Annual production growth of major African resources, by volume, 2008–20, %

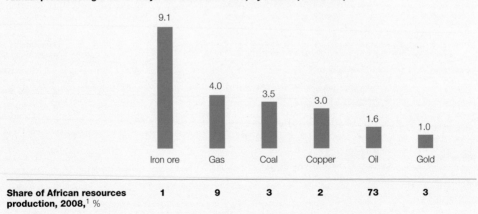

	Iron ore	Gas	Coal	Copper	Oil	Gold
	9.1	4.0	3.5	3.0	1.6	1.0
Share of African resources production, 2008,[1] %	1	9	3	2	73	3

[1] Figures do not sum to 100%, because "other" is not shown.

Source: International Energy Agency; Rand Merchant Bank; McKinsey analysis

Infrastructure: Filling the gap

Africa's massive infrastructure deficit will continue to offer investment opportunities for private players. Comparing Africa with the "BRIC" countries—Brazil, Russia, India, and China—highlights Africa's infrastructure needs. The BRICs' power consumption per capita, for example, is more than twice Africa's. Likewise, the density of road and rail networks in the BRIC countries is about five and two times higher, respectively. (Consequently, logistics costs are up to twice as high in Africa as in the BRICs.)

Fully bridging the gap will be hard. But we calculate that a combination of funding increases and more efficient operations would allow Africa to boost its total infrastructure investment, currently running at around $72 billion a year, by $46 billion annually. This investment level still would leave Africa trailing

the BRICs but would go a long way toward addressing the continent's infrastructure backlog, keeping pace with economic growth, and attaining certain key social targets, such as improving household access to electricity.

Private-sector participation will play a valuable role. We estimate that private investment, along with continued growth in funding from China, could account for more than 40 percent of the new infrastructure spending required by 2013. Private players should partner as operators with governments to help improve the sector's efficiency, as the global companies APM and Cosco do in several of Africa's larger ports. Finally, private financiers should take notice. Those that can effectively diversify, share, and price the investment risk will find large financing opportunities in Africa.

Infrastructure investment, $ billion

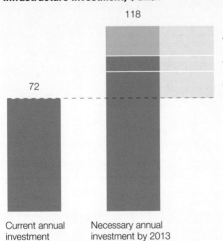

Sources to fill the gap

19 Private-sector investment and China

10 Increased investment from oil-producing countries

17 Operational-efficiency improvements in existing infrastructure (eg, improving efficiency in public utilities by reducing power distribution losses, improving maintenance, and improving bill collection practices)

Current annual investment

Necessary annual investment by 2013

Source: World Bank; McKinsey Global Institute analysis

The authors wish to acknowledge the contributions of their colleagues Tarik Alatovic, Charles Atkins, Mutsa Chironga, Susan Lund, Charles Roxburgh, Amine Tazi-Riffi, Nadia Terfous, Sanya van Schalkwyk, and Till Zeino-Mahmalat.

Norbert Dörr is a director in McKinsey's Johannesburg office, where **Arend van Wamelen** is a principal; **Acha Leke** is a director in the Lagos office.

Establishing priorities in Africa

Mutsa Chironga, Susan Lund, and Charles Roxburgh

 The full version of this article, "What's driving Africa's growth," is available on mckinseyquarterly.com.

Executives and investors eyeing the Africa opportunity clearly can't throw resources at the whole continent. And with GDP growth accelerating in 27 of Africa's 30 largest economies from 2000 to 2008, targeting countries by recent overall performance is too crude for establishing priorities. More useful, we argue, is to consider the economic structure of countries by looking at the degree to which they have expanded into manufacturing and services, as well as their ability to generate export earnings to finance investments. The exhibit below evaluates the prospects of Africa's largest economies against these related goals, using two proxies: the level of economic diversification and exports per capita. Most African countries fall into one of the four clusters shown below. This framework, though imperfect, can not only help guide executives and investors developing strategies for the continent but also offer new perspectives for policy makers working to sustain growth.

Evaluating the prospects of Africa's biggest economies[1]

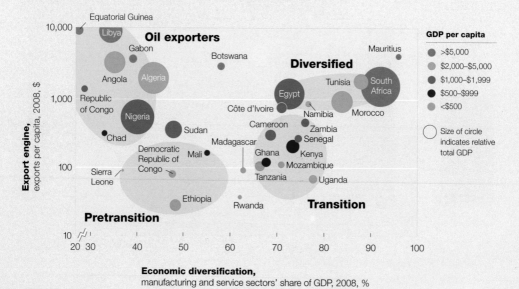

[1] Includes countries with 2008 GDP ≥$10 billion or real GDP growth rate of ≥7% from 2000–08; excludes 22 countries that accounted for 3% of African GDP in 2008.

Source: Organisation for Economic Co-operation and Development (OECD); World Development Indicators, World Bank; McKinsey Global Institute analysis

Diversified economies

Egypt
Morocco
South Africa
Tunisia

Africa's most developed economies and most stable sources of growth are the diversified economies. Over the past decade, their service sectors—including banking, construction, retailing, and telecom—accounted for more than 70 percent of their GDP growth. Their cities have gained more than ten million new residents since 2000, and real consumer spending grew by 3 to 5 percent a year. Today, 90 percent of all households in these economies have some discretionary income. Yet these countries have higher unit labor costs than China or India do and must move to compete in higher-value industries.

Oil exporters

Algeria
Angola
Chad
Equatorial Guinea
Gabon
Libya
Nigeria
Republic of Congo

These countries have Africa's highest GDP per capita but also its least diversified economies, with growth tightly linked to oil and gas prices. Their longer-term growth prospects depend on their ability to use oil wealth to finance broader development. In Nigeria, for example, banking and telecom are booming thanks to economic reforms. Africa's petroleum exporters must invest further in basic infrastructure and education, and maintain political momentum for reform.

Transition economies

Cameroon
Ghana
Kenya
Mozambique
Senegal
Tanzania
Uganda
Zambia

Africa's transition economies are growing rapidly, albeit from a lower base than those of the diversified economies. While agriculture still accounts for two-thirds of their exports, they increasingly sell processed fuels and foods, chemicals, apparel, and cosmetics—particularly to other parts of Africa. With better infrastructure and regulatory systems, these countries could compete with low-cost emerging economies elsewhere. Their service sectors are also growing briskly, though penetration rates in banking, formal retailing, and telecom remain low, creating opportunities for businesses that can satisfy unmet demand.

Pretransition economies

Democratic Republic of Congo
Ethiopia
Mali
Sierra Leone

These countries are very poor; some are just emerging from years of devastating conflict. While they differ greatly, their common problem is a lack of basics such as strong, stable governments and public institutions; good macroeconomics; and sustainable agricultural development. Their key challenges include maintaining political stability, establishing economic basics, and creating a more predictable business environment. Some global companies are already reaping high returns on investments in these economies. With improved economic stability, a number of them could begin tapping their vast natural resources to finance growth.

The authors wish to acknowledge the contributions of their colleagues Tarik Alatovic, Charles Atkins, Norbert Dörr, Acha Leke, Amine Tazi-Riffi, Nadia Terfous, Sanya van Schalkwyk, Arend van Wamelen, and Till Zeino-Mahmalat.

Mutsa Chironga is a consultant in McKinsey's Johannesburg office; **Susan Lund** is director of research at the McKinsey Global Institute, where **Charles Roxburgh** is the London-based director.

How we do it: Three executives offer advice on competing in Africa

William Egbe,
president
of Coca-Cola
South Africa

Jacko Maree,
CEO of
Standard Bank
Group

Maria Ramos,
CEO of Absa

Support socioeconomic development: William Egbe

We have operations in every single country on the continent, even some that do not have governments, like Somalia. People ask, "How does that work?" It works because you understand that you can create a business opportunity, and people can see beyond the politics to engage around the business opportunities. The other reason it works is because you engage local investors in those businesses, to participate in the spoils.

That's very fundamental to have a sustainable business. Multinationals cannot operate in Africa without ensuring that they're building the business system that enables the communities in which they do business to benefit, to thrive and prosper, but also that the locals have a significant stake in those businesses. You actually have a much more valuable business system when you have partners along the value chain who have a vested interest in the long-term survival of your business because they derive a living from your business system. That is the ultimate formula for sustainability on the continent. It doesn't make sense to try to keep all of the gains for yourself.

Companies also have to understand that to have a license to operate in Africa, they have to earn that license, not from the governments but from the consumers. And that license means that you're doing things that support socioeconomic development. You have a role in doing things to support the improvement of the standard of living of Africans. It means that you have to invest in the communities in which you do business—creating jobs, providing skills, providing business opportunities.

Entrepreneurship is critical. For businesses to be able to reduce poverty in Africa, it's not going to come from big companies creating jobs. There's no economy where the bulk of the job creation comes from big companies. It comes from small and medium enterprise.

" Companies have to understand that to have a license to operate in Africa, they have to earn that license, not from the governments but from the consumers. **"**

William Egbe is the president of Coca-Cola South Africa. Before joining Coca-Cola, in 1997, he worked for Eastman Kodak in the United States and Germany.

And if you dig a little bit deeper in entrepreneurship, one aspect that large companies tend to overlook is around supporting female entrepreneurs. We found that, for example, when we wanted to set up small entrepreneurs to help us with our distribution, the failure rate for the businesses that were run by women was half of the rate of the businesses run by men. We also discovered that the female owners of these minor distribution centers were better able to retain their employees. They had lower turnover than the male owners. So when we start looking at what the sweet spots in which we're going to focus our investment to accelerate development in Africa are, we have to look at some of these areas.

For more from William Egbe, watch the executive panel discussion "Can Africa continue to grow?" on mckinseyquarterly.com.

Understand the local environment: Jacko Maree

There are risks to doing business in Africa, but no more so than in some of the Latin American economies or even Russia and Asia. The question is how to manage those risks once you've understood them. We spend a huge amount of time coming to grips with the particular risks that may occur in some of these countries and then try to mitigate them.

Understanding risk is more than just a financial concern. One has to be mindful of ensuring that you're seen as being helpful and relevant to the local economies rather than just extracting profits by providing a service. When you're dealing with developing countries, the issue of the social relevance of your company is completely different from when you're dealing

" The most important question for multinationals is, 'Are you going it alone or are you going to work with partners?' "

Jacko Maree has served as CEO of Standard Bank Group, Africa's largest financial institution by assets, since 1999. A former chairman of the Banking Association South Africa, he is a director of Liberty Life.

with a developed economy. For banks, more so than other enterprises, the question that often comes up when you are visiting government officials or major corporate customers is, "What are you doing for our country?" A bank cannot typically turn around and say, "Well, we're just here to help you with your transactions or your financing requirements." You have to be involved and committed to the communities in which you operate.

The most important question for multinationals is, "Are you going it alone or are you going to work with partners?" Sometimes, having a local partner is really the most obvious way to go. Clearly, you always need advice from someone who understands the local environment. In a number of the countries in which we operate, we have chosen to work in formal partnerships. In some geographies, we have tried to position ourselves first as a local player and second as a multinational.

For major multinationals looking to expand on the African continent, a key question is whether you have sufficient resources to tackle the challenge. What we have found in a number of these countries is that, initially, you've got to use quite a lot of your own resources rather than rely on local skills. Over time, of course, that changes.

For more from Jacko Maree, see "The China–Africa business connection: An interview with the CEO of Standard Bank," on mckinseyquarterly.com.

Expect no shortcuts: Maria Ramos

The first piece of advice I give our teams—and remind myself of—is that we need to do very thorough due diligence. We need to understand that if we are going to invest in another country, we must understand that environment well, irrespective of whether you're investing in Africa or investing in any other geography.

You are going to find some challenges in Africa that you probably wouldn't be finding if you were investing in, for example, parts of Europe. There certainly will be challenges in some aspects of infrastructure and in tele-communications—the World Bank says that African countries lag behind their peers in other parts of the developing world by just about every measure of infrastructure coverage. If you do encounter challenges, what's required is a thorough engagement and commitment to the investment you're making.

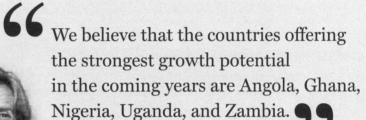

" We believe that the countries offering the strongest growth potential in the coming years are Angola, Ghana, Nigeria, Uganda, and Zambia. "

Maria Ramos is the CEO of Absa, one of South Africa's largest financial-services companies. Before joining Absa, in 2009, Ramos was CEO of Transnet, South Africa's state-owned transport and logistics company.

Sometimes investments have longer return horizons than they do at other times, and that requires you to put some of your best people, technology, and systems on the job. There are no shortcuts. This is not one of those places where you're going to come in and make a quick buck and leave. That said, we believe that the countries offering the strongest growth potential in the coming years are Angola, Ghana, Nigeria, Uganda, and Zambia, which are likely to be the biggest gainers from development in the mining, energy, and other infrastructure sectors. o

For more from Maria Ramos, see "Assessing Africa's business future: An interview with the CEO of Absa," on mckinseyquarterly.com.

Richard Dobbs, Bill Huyett,
and Tim Koller

The CEO's
guide
to corporate
finance

The problem
Strategic decisions can be complicated by competing, often spurious notions of what creates value. Even executives with solid instincts can be seduced by the allure of financial engineering, high leverage, or the idea that well-established rules of economics no longer apply.

Why it matters
Such misconceptions can undermine strategic decision making and slow down economies.

What you should do about it
Test decisions such as whether to undertake acquisitions, make divestitures, invest in projects, or increase executive compensation against four enduring principles of corporate finance. Doing so will often require managers to adopt new practices, such as justifying mergers on the basis of their impact on cash flows rather than on earnings per share, holding regular business exit reviews, focusing on enterprise-wide risks that may lurk within individual projects, and indexing executive compensation to the growth and market performance of peer companies.

Four principles can help you make great financial decisions— even when the CFO's not in the room.

It's one thing for a CFO to understand the technical methods of valuation—and for members of the finance organization to apply them to help line managers monitor and improve company performance. But it's still more powerful when CEOs, board members, and other non-financial executives internalize the principles of value creation. Doing so allows them to make independent, courageous, and even un-popular business decisions in the face of myths and misconceptions about what creates value.

When an organization's senior leaders have a strong financial compass, it's easier for them to resist the siren songs of financial engineering, excessive leverage, and the idea (common during boom times) that somehow the established rules of economics no longer apply. Misconceptions like these—which can lead companies to make value-destroying decisions and slow down entire economies—take hold with surprising and disturbing ease.

What we hope to do in this article is show how four principles, or corner-stones, can help senior executives and board members make some of their most important decisions. The four cornerstones are disarmingly simple:

1. The core-of-value principle establishes that value creation is a function of returns on capital and growth, while highlighting some important subtleties associated with applying these concepts.

2. The conservation-of-value principle says that it doesn't matter how you slice the financial pie with financial engineering, share repurchases, or acquisitions; only improving cash flows will create value.

3. The expectations treadmill principle explains how movements in a company's share price reflect changes in the stock market's expectations about performance, not just the company's actual performance (in terms of growth and returns on invested capital). The higher those expectations, the better that company must perform just to keep up.

4. The best-owner principle states that no business has an inherent value in and of itself; it has a different value to different owners or potential owners—a value based on how they manage it and what strategy they pursue.

Ignoring these cornerstones can lead to poor decisions that erode the value of companies. Consider what happened during the run-up to the financial crisis that began in 2007. Participants in the securitized-mortgage market all assumed that securitizing risky home loans made them more valuable because it reduced the risk of the assets. But this notion violates the conservation-of-value rule. Securitization did not increase the aggregated cash flows of the home loans, so no value was created, and the initial risks remained. Securitizing the assets simply enabled the risks

Give each business unit a date stamp,
or estimated time of exit, and review them
regularly. This keeps exits on the agenda
and obliges executives to evaluate businesses
as their "sell-by date" approaches.

to be passed on to other owners: some investors, somewhere, had to be
holding them.

Obvious as this seems in hindsight, a great many smart people missed it
at the time. And the same thing happens every day in executive suites and
board rooms as managers and company directors evaluate acquisitions,
divestitures, projects, and executive compensation. As we'll see, the four
cornerstones of finance provide a perennially stable frame of reference
for managerial decisions like these.

Mergers and acquisitions

Acquisitions are both an important source of growth for companies and
an important element of a dynamic economy. Acquisitions that put
companies in the hands of better owners or managers or that reduce excess
capacity typically create substantial value both for the economy as a
whole and for investors.

You can see this effect in the increased combined cash flows of the many
companies involved in acquisitions. But although they create value overall,
the distribution of that value tends to be lopsided, accruing primarily
to the selling companies' shareholders. In fact, most empirical research
shows that just half of the acquiring companies create value for their
own shareholders.

The conservation-of-value principle is an excellent reality check for
executives who want to make sure their acquisitions create value for their
shareholders. The principle reminds us that acquisitions create value
when the cash flows of the combined companies are greater than they
would otherwise have been. Some of that value will accrue to the
acquirer's shareholders if it doesn't pay too much for the acquisition.

Exhibit 1 shows how this process works. Company A buys Company B for
$1.3 billion—a transaction that includes a 30 percent premium over its
market value. Company A expects to increase the value of Company B by

40 percent through various operating improvements, so the value of
Company B to Company A is $1.4 billion. Subtracting the purchase price
of $1.3 billion from $1.4 billion leaves $100 million of value creation
for Company A's shareholders.

In other words, when the stand-alone value of the target equals the market
value, the acquirer creates value for its shareholders only when the value
of improvements is greater than the premium paid. With this in mind, it's
easy to see why most of the value creation from acquisitions goes to
the sellers' shareholders: if a company pays a 30 percent premium, it must
increase the target's value by at least 30 percent to create any value.

While a 30 or 40 percent performance improvement sounds steep, that's
what acquirers often achieve. For example, Exhibit 2 highlights four
large deals in the consumer products sector. Performance improvements
typically exceeded 50 percent of the target's value.

Our example also shows why it's difficult for an acquirer to create a
substantial amount of value from acquisitions. Let's assume that
Company A was worth about three times Company B at the time of the
acquisition. Significant as such a deal would be, it's likely to increase
Company A's value by only 3 percent—the $100 million of value creation
depicted in Exhibit 1, divided by Company A's value, $3 billion.

**To create value, an acquirer must achieve performance improvements
that are greater than the premium paid.**

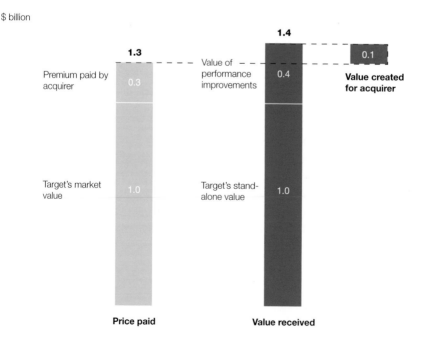

Dramatic performance improvement created significant value in these four acquisitions.

	Present value of announced performance improvements as a % of target's stand-alone value	Premium paid as a % of target's stand-alone value	Net value created from acquisition as a % of purchase price
Kellogg acquires Keebler (2000)	45–70	15	30–50
PepsiCo acquires Quaker Oats (2000)	35–55	10	25–40
Clorox acquires First Brands (1998)	70–105	60	5–25
Henkel acquires National Starch (2007)	60–90	55	5–25

Finally, it's worth noting that we have not mentioned an acquisition's effect on earnings per share (EPS). Although this metric is often considered, no empirical link shows that expected EPS accretion or dilution is an important indicator of whether an acquisition will create or destroy value. Deals that strengthen near-term EPS and deals that dilute near-term EPS are equally likely to create or destroy value. Bankers and other finance professionals know all this, but as one told us recently, many nonetheless "use it as a simple way to communicate with boards of directors." To avoid confusion during such communications, executives should remind themselves and their colleagues that EPS has nothing to say about which company is the best owner of specific corporate assets or about how merging two entities will change the cash flows they generate.

Divestitures

Executives are often concerned that divestitures will look like an admission of failure, make their company smaller, and reduce its stock market value. Yet the research shows that, on the contrary, the stock market consistently reacts positively to divestiture announcements.[1] The divested business units also benefit. Research has shown that the profit margins of spun-off businesses tend to increase by one-third during the three years after the transactions are complete.[2]

These findings illustrate the benefit of continually applying the best-owner principle: the attractiveness of a business and its best owner will

---

[1] J. Mulherin and Audra Boone, "Comparing acquisitions and divestitures," *Journal of Corporate Finance*, 2000, Volume 6, Number 2, pp. 117–39.
[2] Patrick Cusatis, James Miles, and J. Woolridge, "Some new evidence that spinoffs create value," *Journal of Applied Corporate Finance*, 1994, Volume 7, Number 2, pp. 100–107.

probably change over time. At different stages of an industry's or
company's lifespan, resource decisions that once made economic sense
can become problematic. For instance, the company that invented a
groundbreaking innovation may not be best suited to exploit it. Similarly,
as demand falls off in a mature industry, companies that have been in it
a long time are likely to have excess capacity and therefore may no longer
be the best owners.

A value-creating approach to divestitures can lead to the pruning of good
and bad businesses at any stage of their life cycles. Clearly, divesting
a good business is often not an intuitive choice and may be difficult for
managers—even if that business would be better owned by another
company. It therefore makes sense to enforce some discipline in active
portfolio management. One way to do so is to hold regular review
meetings specifically devoted to business exits, ensuring that the topic
remains on the executive agenda and that each unit receives a date stamp,
or estimated time of exit. This practice has the advantage of obliging
executives to evaluate all businesses as the "sell-by date" approaches.

Executives and boards often worry that divestitures will reduce their
company's size and thus cut its value in the capital markets. There follows
a misconception that the markets value larger companies more than
smaller ones. But this notion holds only for very small firms, with some
evidence that companies with a market capitalization of less than
$500 million might have slightly higher costs of capital.[3]

Finally, executives shouldn't worry that a divestiture will dilute EPS
multiples. A company selling a business with a lower P/E ratio than that
of its remaining businesses will see an overall reduction in earnings
per share. But don't forget that a divested underperforming unit's lower
growth and ROIC potential would have previously depressed the entire
company's P/E. With this unit gone, the company that remains will have a
higher growth and ROIC potential—and will be valued at a corre-
spondingly higher P/E ratio.[4] As the core-of-value principle would predict,

[3] See Robert S. McNish and Michael W. Palys, "Does scale matter to capital markets?"
McKinsey on Finance, Number 16, Summer 2005, pp. 21–23 (also available on
mckinseyquarterly.com).
[4] Similarly, if a company sells a unit with a high P/E relative to its other units, the earnings
per share (EPS) will increase but the P/E will decline proportionately.

financial mechanics, on their own, do not create or destroy value. By the way, the math works out regardless of whether the proceeds from a sale are used to pay down debt or to repurchase shares. What matters for value is the business logic of the divestiture.

Project analysis and downside risks

Reviewing the financial attractiveness of project proposals is a common task for senior executives. The sophisticated tools used to support them—discounted cash flows, scenario analyses—often lull top management into a false sense of security. For example, one company we know analyzed projects by using advanced statistical techniques that always showed a zero probability of a project with negative net present value (NPV). The organization did not have the ability to discuss failure, only varying degrees of success.

Such an approach ignores the core-of-value principle's laserlike focus on the future cash flows underlying returns on capital and growth, not just for a project but for the enterprise as a whole. Actively considering downside risks to future cash flows for both is a crucial subtlety of project analysis—and one that often isn't undertaken.

For a moment, put yourself in the mind of an executive deciding whether to undertake a project with an upside of $80 million, a downside of –$20 million, and an expected value of $60 million. Generally accepted finance theory says that companies should take on all projects with a positive expected value, regardless of the upside-versus-downside risk.

But what if the downside would bankrupt the company? That might be the case for an electric-power utility considering the construction of a nuclear facility for $15 billion (a rough 2009 estimate for a facility with two reactors). Suppose there is an 80 percent chance the plant will be successfully constructed, brought in on time, and worth, net of investment costs, $13 billion. Suppose further that there is also a 20 percent chance that the utility company will fail to receive regulatory approval to start operating the new facility, which will then be worth –$15 billion. That means the net expected value of the facility is more than $7 billion—seemingly an attractive investment.[5]

The decision gets more complicated if the cash flow from the company's existing plants will be insufficient to cover its existing debt plus the debt on the new plant if it fails. The economics of the nuclear plant will then spill over into the value of the rest of the company—which has

---

[5] The expected value is $7.4 billion, which represents the sum of 80 percent of $13 billion ($28 billion, the expected value of the plant, less the $15 billion investment) and 20 percent of –$15 billion ($0, less the $15 billion investment).

$25 billion in existing debt and $25 billion in equity market capitalization. Failure will wipe out all the company's equity, not just the $15 billion invested in the plant.

As this example makes clear, we can extend the core-of-value principle to say that a company should not take on a risk that will put its future cash flows in danger. In other words, don't do anything that has large negative spillover effects on the rest of the company. This caveat should be enough to guide managers in the earlier example of a project with an $80 million upside, a –$20 million downside, and a $60 million expected value. If a $20 million loss would endanger the company as a whole, the managers should forgo the project. On the other hand, if the project doesn't endanger the company, they should be willing to risk the $20 million loss for a far greater potential gain.

Executive compensation

Establishing performance-based compensation systems is a daunting task, both for board directors concerned with the CEO and the senior team and for human-resource leaders and other executives focused on, say, the top 500 managers. Although an entire industry has grown up around the compensation of executives, many companies continue to reward them for short-term total returns to shareholders (TRS). TRS, however, is driven more by movements in a company's industry and in the broader market (or by stock market expectations) than by individual performance. For example, many executives who became wealthy from stock options during the 1980s and 1990s saw these gains wiped out in 2008. Yet the underlying causes of share price changes—such as falling interest rates in the earlier period and the financial crisis more recently—were frequently disconnected from anything managers did or didn't do.

Using TRS as the basis of executive compensation reflects a fundamental misunderstanding of the third cornerstone of finance: the expectations treadmill. If investors have low expectations for a company at the beginning of a period of stock market growth, it may be relatively easy for the company's managers to beat them. But that also increases the expectations of new shareholders, so the company has to improve ever faster just to keep up and maintain its new stock price. At some point, it becomes difficult if not impossible for managers to deliver on these accelerating expectations without faltering, much as anyone would eventually stumble on a treadmill that kept getting faster.

This dynamic underscores why it's difficult to use TRS as a performance-measurement tool: extraordinary managers may deliver only ordinary TRS because it is extremely difficult to keep beating ever-higher share price expectations. Conversely, if markets have low performance expectations for a company, its managers might find it easy to earn a high TRS, at least for a short time, by raising market expectations up to the level for its peers.

Instead, compensation programs should focus on growth, returns on capital, and TRS performance, relative to peers (an important point) rather than an absolute target. That approach would eliminate much of the TRS that is not driven by company-specific performance. Such a solution sounds simple but, until recently, was made impractical by accounting rules and, in some countries, tax policies. Prior to 2004, for example, companies using US generally accepted accounting principles (GAAP) could avoid listing stock options as an expense on their income statements provided they met certain criteria, one of which was that the exercise price had to be fixed. To avoid taking an earnings hit, companies avoided compensation systems based on relative performance, which would have required more flexibility in structuring options.

Since 2004, a few companies have moved to share-based compensation systems tied to relative performance. GE, for one, granted its CEO a performance award based on the company's TRS relative to the TRS of the S&P 500 index. We hope that more companies will follow this direction.

●　　●　　●

Applying the four cornerstones of finance sometimes means going against the crowd. It means accepting that there are no free lunches. It means relying on data, thoughtful analysis, and a deep understanding of the competitive dynamics of an industry. None of this is easy, but the payoff—the creation of value for a company's stakeholders and for society at large—is enormous. ○

Richard Dobbs is a director in McKinsey's Seoul office and a director of the McKinsey Global Institute; **Bill Huyett** is a director in the Boston office; and **Tim Koller** is a principal in the New York office. This article has been excerpted from *Value: The Four Cornerstones of Corporate Finance*, by Richard Dobbs, Bill Huyett, and Tim Koller (Wiley, October 2010). Koller is also a coauthor of *Valuation: Measuring and Managing the Value of Companies* (fifth edition, Wiley, July 2010).

For a stand-alone summary of this article's principles and how to apply them, see "The four cornerstones of corporate finance," on page 112.

Joanna Barsh, Josephine
Mogelof, and Caroline Webb

How centered leaders achieve extraordinary results

Artwork by Gwenda Kaczor

Executives can thrive at
work and in life by adopting a
leadership model that
revolves around finding their
strengths and connecting
with others.

One senior manager's harrowing moment of truth, on page 89.

The problem
Today's complex, volatile, and fast-paced business environment is placing extraordinary stress on leaders.

Why it matters
Many leaders lack the skills needed to cope, which undermines organizational performance and personal satisfaction.

What you should do about it
Cultivate the capabilities we have identified in research on leaders who can unlock the organization's potential in challenging circumstances:

Give your life and work a sense of meaning that you communicate openly to others.

Frame challenges constructively, emphasizing opportunities in change and uncertainty.

Tap a broad constellation of internal and external constituents who can help your organization succeed.

Engage proactively with risks and help your organization do the same.

Sustain your energy while creating the conditions for others to restore theirs.

For the past six years, we have been on a journey to learn from leaders who are able to find the best in themselves and in turn inspire, engage, and mobilize others, even in the most demanding circumstances. And the business environment *has* become more demanding: the global financial crisis and subsequent economic downturn have ratcheted up the pressure on leaders already grappling with a world in transformation. More than half of the CEOs we and our colleagues have spoken with in the past year have said that their organization must fundamentally rethink its business model.

Our work can help. We have conducted interviews with more than 140 leaders; analysis of a wide range of academic research in fields as diverse as organizational development, evolutionary biology, neuroscience, positive psychology, and leadership; workshops with hundreds of clients to test our ideas; and global surveys. Through this research, we distilled a set of five capabilities that, in combination, generate high levels of professional performance and life satisfaction. We described this set of capabilities, which we call "centered leadership," in the *Quarterly* in 2008 and subsequently in a book, *How Remarkable Women Lead.*[1] Since then, through additional interviews and quantitative research, we've continued to validate the model's applicability to leaders across different regions, cultures, and seniority levels. Better yet, we have confirmed that centered leadership appears equally useful to men. In other words, it is not just for women, but for all leaders in demanding circumstances.

Five capabilities are at the heart of centered leadership: finding meaning in work, converting emotions such as fear or stress into opportunity, leveraging connections and community, acting in the face of risk, and sustaining the energy that is the life force of change. A recent McKinsey global survey of executives shows that leaders who have mastered even one of these skills are twice as likely as those who have mastered none to feel that they can lead through change; masters of all five are more than four times as likely.[2] Strikingly, leaders who have mastered all five capabilities are also more than 20 times as likely to say they are satisfied with their performance as leaders and their lives in general.

For more on the research, see sidebar, "The value of centered leadership," on page 82.

[1] Joanna Barsh, Susie Cranston, and Geoffrey Lewis, *How Remarkable Women Lead: The Breakthrough Model for Work and Life*, New York: Crown Business Publishing, 2009.
[2] The online survey was in the field from July 6 to 16, 2010. It garnered responses from 2,498 executives representing all regions, industries, functional specialties, and tenures. Respondents indicated their level of agreement with statements representing various dimensions of the leadership model. We then aggregated their answers into degrees of mastery of each dimension.

Five dimensions of centered leadership

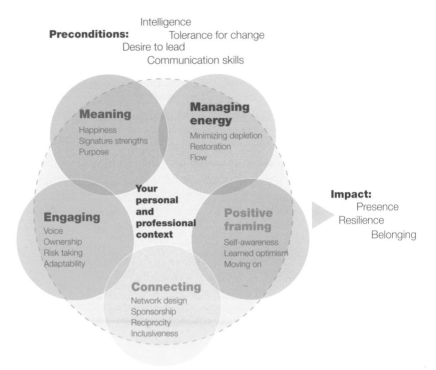

Preconditions: Intelligence
Tolerance for change
Desire to lead
Communication skills

Meaning
Happiness
Signature strengths
Purpose

Managing energy
Minimizing depletion
Restoration
Flow

Your personal and professional context

Engaging
Voice
Ownership
Risk taking
Adaptability

Positive framing
Self-awareness
Learned optimism
Moving on

Connecting
Network design
Sponsorship
Reciprocity
Inclusiveness

Impact: Presence
Resilience
Belonging

While such results help make the case for centered leadership, executives seeking to enhance their leadership performance and general satisfaction often find personal stories more tangible. Accordingly, as this article revisits the five dimensions of centered leadership—and their applicability to times of uncertainty, stress, and change—we share the experiences of four men and one woman, all current or former CEOs of major global corporations.

Meaning

We all recognize leaders who infuse their life and work with a sense of meaning. They convey energy and enthusiasm because the goal is important to them personally, because they are actively enjoying its pursuit, and because their work plays to their strengths. Our survey results show that, of all the dimensions of centered leadership, meaning has a significant impact on satisfaction with both work and life; indeed, its contribution to general life satisfaction is five times more powerful than that of any other dimension.

Whatever the source of meaning (and it can differ dramatically from one person to another), centered leaders often talk about how their purpose appeals to something greater than themselves and the importance of

(Continued on page 84)

The value of centered leadership:
About the research

This article rests in part on the results of our latest survey on centered leadership.[1] We asked more than 2,000 executives around the world questions that allowed us to assess their mastery of the five dimensions of centered leadership and how satisfied they are with their professional leadership and their lives overall.

We found that men and women are very similar in the degree to which they practice the elements of centered leadership and experience satisfaction in their work performance and their lives (Exhibit 1). Further, among the 29 questions that we used to assess mastery of each dimension,

there were statistically significant differences between men and women on only 11, and those differences were minimal. (For our purposes, respondents master each dimension when their answers put them in the top 20 percent of overall scores.)

Women do have a slight edge: they have a higher share of the top quintile than of the overall pool, suggesting that centered leadership remains geared to women's strengths.[2] That a very high share of men have mastered each dimension shows, however, that centered leadership is not about being a woman but rather about abilities, mind-sets, and behaviors

Exhibit 1

Men and women alike can master the dimensions of centered leadership and feel successful in both their performance at work and their lives.

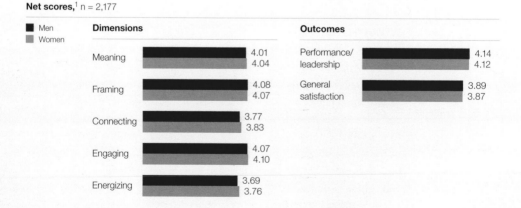

Net scores,[1] n = 2,177

- Men
- Women

Dimensions		Outcomes	
Meaning	4.01 / 4.04	Performance/ leadership	4.14 / 4.12
Framing	4.08 / 4.07	General satisfaction	3.89 / 3.87
Connecting	3.77 / 3.83		
Engaging	4.07 / 4.10		
Energizing	3.69 / 3.76		

[1] All results are mean scores calculated on a 5-point scale, where 5 is equal to "strongly agree."

sometimes considered feminine, such as being motivated by meaning at work—as opposed to pay or status—and seeking to forge community and collaboration.

The results also make it clear that there is a tight relationship between mastery of centered leadership and the self-assessed performance of executives as leaders and their satisfaction with life in general. Notably, the more of the relevant dimensions leaders master, the likelier they are to be very satisfied with their performance (Exhibit 2).

Finally, we observed that the youngest respondents—both men and women—were least likely to have mastered any dimension except connecting. This suggests that young people seeking to become leaders would benefit significantly from undertaking the centered-leadership journey sooner rather than later. Further, companies that support their young executives in doing so will reap the benefits, such as higher performance and greater corporate resilience, earlier.

[1] For more, see "The value of centered leadership: McKinsey Global Survey results," to be published in the fall of 2010 on mckinseyquarterly.com.
[2] Women made up 35 percent of the total sample; the shares of women who have mastered the various dimensions range from 34 to 41 percent, with four of the five above 35 percent.

Exhibit 2

The more of the relevant dimensions leaders master, the likelier they are to be very satisfied with their performance.

% of respondents

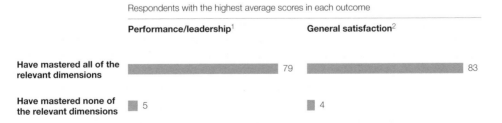

Respondents with the highest average scores in each outcome

	Performance/leadership[1]	General satisfaction[2]
Have mastered all of the relevant dimensions	79	83
Have mastered none of the relevant dimensions	5	4

[1] For performance/leadership, the 4 dimensions that have a meaningful impact on outcome scores are, in order of descending influence, meaning, engaging, framing, and connecting; for "mastered all," n = 106; for "mastered none," n = 1,302.
[2] For general satisfaction, the 4 dimensions that have a meaningful impact on outcome scores are, in order of descending influence, meaning, energizing, engaging, and connecting; for "mastered all," n = 103; for "mastered none," n = 1,258.

conveying their passion to others (for more on conveying meaning to others, see "Revealing your moment of truth," on page 89). Time and again, we heard that sharing meaning to inspire colleagues requires leaders to become great storytellers, touching hearts as well as minds. These skills are particularly applicable for executives leading through major transitions, since it takes strong personal motivation to triumph over the discomfort and fear that accompany change and that can drown out formal corporate messages, which in any event rarely fire the souls of employees and inspire greater achievement.

Avon Products CEO Andrea Jung described how meaning and storytelling came together when her company faltered after years of rapid growth. Andrea's personal challenge was acute because some key sources of her passion—creating a bold vision for growth and inspiring others to dream big, being a member of a close-knit community, and achieving extraordinary results—were deeply connected with her work at Avon. Suddenly, it became harder for her to see where her momentum would come from. What's more, she had to streamline her cherished community.

To remain true to her personal values, Andrea rejected the "more efficient" approach of delegating to managers the responsibility for communicating with employees about the restructuring and of sharing information only on a need-to-know basis. Instead, she traveled the world to offer her teams a vision for restoring growth and to share the difficult decisions that would be required to secure the company's future. The result? Employees felt that Andrea treated them with honesty and humanity, making the harsh reality of job reductions easier to accept and giving them more time to prepare. They also experienced her love for the company firsthand and recognized that both she and Avon were doing all they could. By instilling greater resilience throughout the organization, Avon rebuilt its community and resumed growth within 18 months.

Positive framing

Positive psychologists have shown that some people tend to frame the world optimistically, others pessimistically.[3] Optimists often have an edge: in our survey, three-quarters of the respondents who were particularly good at positive framing thought they had the right skills to lead change, while only 15 percent of those who weren't thought so.

For leaders who don't naturally see opportunity in change and uncertainty, those conditions create stress. When faced with too much stress (each of us has a different limit), the brain reacts with a modern version of the "fight, flight, or freeze" instinct that saber-toothed tigers inspired in early

[3]Martin E. P. Seligman, *Authentic Happiness: Using the New Positive Psychology to Realize Your Potential for Lasting Fulfillment*, New York, NY: Free Press, 2004.

humans. This response equips us only for survival, not for coming up with creative solutions. Worse yet, in organizations such behavior feeds on itself, breeding fear and negativity that can spread and become the cultural norm.

When Steve Sadove took over Clairol, in 1991, for example, the company had been shell-shocked by a significant decline in sales volume. "I remember going to a very creative person, who did all the packaging and creative development," Steve told us, "and saying, 'Why don't we do anything creative?' He opened some drawers in his desk and started showing me all of this wonderful work that he'd done. Nobody was asking for it; people kept their head down in that culture. So part of my role as the leader was to create an environment that was going to allow innovation and creativity and make it OK to fail."

Fortunately, we can all become aware of what triggers our fears and learn to work through them to reframe what is happening more constructively. Once we have mastered reframing, we can help others learn this skill, seeding the conditions that result in a safe environment where all employees are inspired to give their best.[4]

Steve found ways to stimulate creativity, such as exploring opposing points of view in discussions with colleagues. Over time, he convinced others that speaking up wasn't just tolerated but encouraged. He helped colleagues reframe the way they reacted to dissent, forging a less defensive and ultimately more innovative culture. Steve and his team introduced a winning hair care brand, Herbal Essences, and ushered in a golden period of growth for Clairol.

Connecting

With communications traveling at warp speed, simple hierarchical cascades—from the CEO down until the chain breaks—are becoming less and less effective for leaders. For starters, leaders depend increasingly on their ability to manage complex webs of connections that aren't suited to traditional, linear communication styles. Further, leaders can find the volume of communication in such networks overwhelming. While this environment can be challenging, it also allows more people to contribute, generating not only wisdom and a wealth of ideas but also immeasurable commitment.

The upshot: CEOs have always needed to select exemplary leadership teams. Increasingly, they must also be adept at building relationships with people scattered across the ecosystem in which they do business and at

[4]Michael A. Cohn et al., "Happiness unpacked: Positive emotions increase life satisfaction by building resilience," American Psychological Association, *Emotion*, 2009, Volume 9, Number 3, pp. 361–68.

bringing together the right people to offer meaningful input and support in solving problems.

Macy's CEO Terry Lundgren learned firsthand about the power of connecting the internal community in 1988 when, 15 months after joining the retailer Neiman Marcus, he became its president and CEO. Shaking things up was core to his role: "I was one of the first non–Marcus family members with that title for any extended period of time." Employees greeted him with widespread skepticism. "They were all thinking, 'Who is this 37-year-old guy who is going to tell us how we should run our fantastic business?'" So Terry held a town hall meeting in the library across the street from company headquarters, in downtown Dallas. He invited anybody who wanted to come. The first time, he recalls, "I had only about 30 people show up! I thought it was going to be a little bit bigger than that, but I tried to be very direct and use the time mostly to listen and respond." He kept holding meetings, noting that "it really moved the needle quickly in terms of getting things done in that company." By the time Terry left, the twice-a-year meetings filled a 1,200-seat auditorium.

Today, as Terry leads Macy's, he connects the dots internally and externally in many ways, from scheduling a monthly breakfast with new managers to forming relationships with peers who have led companies through change. Terry has also emphasized corporate connectivity, regrouping Macy's stores into 69 districts, each tasked with creating "My Macy's" for its customer base. And comparable-store sales are up this year, reversing a negative trend. Terry's top team believes its efforts to connect managers more closely to one another and to customers, through enhanced information sharing and product offerings tailored to local needs, help explain the company's trajectory.

Engaging

Of survey respondents who indicated they were poor at engaging—with risk, with fear, and even with opportunity—only 13 percent thought they had the skills to lead change. That's hardly surprising: risk aversion and fear run rampant during times of change. Leaders who are good at acknowledging and countering these emotions can help their people summon the courage to act and thus unleash tremendous potential.

But for many leaders, encouraging others to take risks is extremely difficult. The responsibility CEOs feel for the performance of the entire organization can make the very notion of supporting risk taking extremely uncomfortable. What's more, to acknowledge the existence of risk, CEOs must admit they don't, in fact, have all the answers—an unusual mind-set for many leaders whose ascent has been built on a virtuous cycle of success and self-confidence.

Doug Stern, CEO of United Media, has a number of ways to help his people evaluate risks and build their confidence about confronting the unknown. Because he has seen the destructive impact of anxiety, Doug follows an explicit process anytime he's facing a new, risky project (for example, selling some of his company's assets). The process helps everyone—himself included—prepare by devising risk mitigation strategies using these steps:

• asking the team to imagine every bad scenario, even the most remotely possible—what he calls the "darkest nightmares"

• giving everyone a chance to describe those scenarios in detail and then to "peer into the darkness" together

• devising a detailed plan for countering each nightmare—in effect, rehearsing the best collective response to each potential issue

Once fears have surfaced and been dealt with, the team has a protocol in place for every worst possible scenario and a set of next steps to implement.[5]

Managing energy

Sustaining change requires the enthusiasm and commitment of large numbers of people across an organization for an extended period of time. All too often, though, a change effort starts with a big bang of vision statements and detailed initiatives, only to see energy peter out. The opposite, when work escalates maniacally through a culture of "relentless enthusiasm," is equally problematic.[6] Either way, leaders will find it hard to sustain energy and commitment within the organization unless they systemically restore their own energy (physical, mental, emotional, and spiritual), as well as create the conditions and serve as role models for others to do the same. Our research suggests sustaining and restoring energy is something leaders often skimp on.

While stress is often related to work, sometimes simple bad luck is at play, as Jurek Gruhn, president of Novo Nordisk US, can attest. Nine years ago he was diagnosed with Type 1 diabetes. Working for a world leader in diabetes care, Jurek was no stranger to the illness and, along with his optimistic spirit, his no-nonsense orientation became a deep source of energy: "My first reaction was, 'You may have Type 1 diabetes, but you

[5] Psychologist Gary Klein has developed and applied in a variety of settings a similar approach that he calls the "premortem." For more on this technique, and on the broader problem of executive overconfidence, see "Strategic decisions: When can you trust your gut?" mckinseyquarterly.com, March 2010.
[6] Edy Greenblatt, *Restore Yourself: The Antidote for Professional Exhaustion*, Los Angeles, CA: Execu-Care Press, 2009.

could also have a lot of other diseases that are much worse.'" So, he told us, "I went to the hospital for two or three days of testing and then went back home. We had our Christmas break. After that, I was back in the office. My wife, who is a physician, said to me, 'That was a quick process!' I basically took on my disease as a task."

Jurek realized that one key to living a normal life with the disease is to embrace life, at work and at home. "A healthy lifestyle is important. I have five kids: my oldest daughter is 25, and my youngest is 6. Sometimes they completely drain my energy, but they can energize me a lot. And now I feel healthier because I have also changed my lifestyle: I eat breakfast now every day, I exercise much more, and I started rock-climbing on a regular basis." Everything improved—his physical condition, mental focus, emotional satisfaction, and spirit. He even learned to face what drained him most—unhealthy conflict at work—by addressing it directly and quickly, much as he handled his diabetes.

Even for leaders without such a challenge, Jurek sets another valuable example: "I saw this comedian who said that a man's brain is filled with boxes, and one of them is empty. Well, when the day's really tough in the office, I go into my empty box for 10 or 15 minutes and I do nothing. If I completely switch off for a short period of time, I get my energy back. Now, I'm not switching off every 15 minutes after working for 15 minutes— maybe I do it every few days. But I do not work weekends unless I really have to. And I'm not one who wakes up and the first thing is the BlackBerry. No way!"

•   •   •

Centered leadership is a journey, not a destination, and it starts with a highly personal decision. We'll leave you with the words of one executive who recently chose to embark on this path: "Our senior team is always talking about changing the organization, changing the mind-sets and behavior of everyone. Now I see that transformation is not about that. It starts with me and my willingness and ability to transform myself. Only then will others transform." ○

The authors would like to thank Aaron De Smet and Johanne Lavoie for their extraordinary contributions to this work.

Joanna Barsh is a director in McKinsey's New York office, **Josephine Mogelof** is a consultant in the Los Angeles office, and **Caroline Webb** is a principal in the London office.

Revealing your moment of truth

Management thinker Stan Slap argues that the best leaders bring their values to work and shares one senior executive's life-changing story.

Stan Slap

The purpose of leadership isn't to increase shareholder value or the productivity of work teams, though effective leadership does these things. Rather, the purpose of leadership is to change the world around you in the name of your values, so you can live those values more fully and use them to make life better for others. The *process* of leadership is to turn your values into a compelling cause for others.

After all, you can't live your top personal values at work without the support of your people. But could they, without hesitation, pick your values from a long list? Could they describe the benefits of supporting those values? If the answer to either question is no—and for most senior managers it is—then you haven't begun to see the performance your people are capable of.

To change this dynamic, you must reset the standard of what's possible in the relationship between you and your people. In my experience, the best method for accomplishing this objective is to reveal "moments of truth": the stories of how you know your values are real to you, where they came from and how you learned them, and the intimate and profound personal experiences—glorious or traumatic—that shaped your self-awareness.

To pull this feat off, you'll have to step out from behind whatever protection your job title affords and make yourself willingly vulnerable. In doing so, you are saying: "From my experiences, this is what is most important about living." By disclosing how your unshakable view of life priorities was formed, you are offering proof of your commitment to these values. One well-known senior executive took this advice to heart and told her staff about a savage yet triumphant experience that she had never previously revealed to most of her friends—and certainly never to her employees—in a way that underlined just how strongly she felt about her connection to them. This is her story.

One executive's moment of truth

"I grew up in a very small town in the Deep South. There were two schools in our town: the white school and the black school. Since I'm black, I went to the black school, which didn't have as many teachers or books or fun things as the white school. But I was a smart little girl, and my mother made up for the lack of resources when I got home every day. Before I could go out and play, we would sit at the dining-room table, and she would take down a big, old encyclopedia from the shelf and teach me about the world.

"I looked up to see four huge men on horseback with masks on, carrying baseball bats. They were riding right at us."

"One day I brought home a report card that was so good my mother said, 'I think we can get you into the white school. Do you want to go?' 'Yes!' I said, because I was a smart girl and I wanted to learn. I didn't know that the school district was under a lot of federal pressure to integrate. Our family talked about it and decided that if the school would accept me, I would go—as long as my two older brothers transferred with me. My brothers didn't want to go, but they loved their little sister and so they agreed. We would be the first black children at the school.

"I had only two dresses and I got to wear my church dress on my first day in school! I was assigned a seat in the back next to a little redheaded white girl and I immediately became best friends with her, the way little girls do. When the bell rang for recess, I went out to the schoolyard to play with my new friend and her other friends. All of the girls were on the schoolyard, and all of the boys were playing on the football field. A large wire fence separated the two areas. My new friend told me that boys and girls used to play together, but since my two brothers were here now the school had put up the fence to separate the boys from the girls.

"We were playing and screaming and laughing when we heard screaming of a different kind from the edge of the schoolyard. I looked up to see four huge men on horseback with masks on, carrying baseball bats. They were riding right at us. Everyone ran toward the school building. The teachers got there first and locked the doors behind them. As I was running, I could hear my brothers yelling my name. They were clawing at the fence, trying to save me, but the fence was too high.

"I was a fast little girl—weighed almost nothing, and most of it was legs. I was already almost to the bleacher seats stacked against the wall of the school building. I knew if I could scramble under those bleachers, the horses couldn't get to me. I was just about to roll under the seats when I heard a scream I thought I recognized. I turned around and saw that one of the riders had grabbed my new friend by the hair—she had been playing with me—and was holding her a couple of feet off the ground. She was screaming and sobbing.

"I didn't even stop to think. I just turned around and ran at that man on the horse. He was holding my friend on the left side of the horse. This horse was so big and it was sweating and its eyes were wild and glaring at me. It was trying to move around to kick me. I ran to the man's right side and sunk my teeth into his leg, biting him as hard as I could.

"The good news is that he dropped my friend, but he picked me up instead. He dragged me by my arm across the concrete and two blocks outside the schoolyard. My Sunday dress got torn off. I was bruised all over, the skin on my back and side and left leg was in ribbons, and they told me that I lost a lot of blood. He left me lying in the street, but I don't really remember that.

"My mother came to the hospital every day for five weeks. Every day, she brought my school lessons and that old encyclopedia and she would help me study the best I could. When I got out, she asked me what I wanted to do. 'I want to go back to the white school and graduate,' I said. And I did.

"I am a grown woman now. I am a successful executive. I am a wife and I am a mother. In this life, I have had an opportunity to learn what is most important to me, and what is most important to me is loyalty. The little white girl from that school is still my best friend today. I'm not willing to live without loyalty in my life and I'm not willing to have people I care about live without it.

"We have a lot of pressures on our team these days. You're working very hard, and we often don't get the cooperation we need from other departments. Things aren't always easy for us, and I know that. I know this will change, because we will be the ones to change it. I just can't tell you when it will change.

"But I can tell you this: if you are working for me and you ever get into trouble trying to do the right thing—I'm coming back for you."

Postscript

As I've observed time and again in working with companies around the world, taking the risk to share a "moment of truth" can help make leaders better and produce real business benefits. But what if your story isn't as jaw-dropping as this one?

The answer is that your story doesn't have to be dramatic, only real. True epiphanies often come from a series of small moments—visible, for instance, only after reflecting on the decisions that first caused you to need your values or become aware of them. Indeed, simply looking at your values consciously often helps connect them to the specific moments—big or small—that made a difference to you then and can again now. o

Stan Slap is the author of *Bury My Heart at Conference Room B: The Unbeatable Impact of Truly Committed Managers* (Portfolio, 2010), from which this article was adapted.

Applied Insight

Tools, techniques, and frameworks for managers

A culture of knowledge sharing and collaboration can improve the quality of scientific work.

Boosting the productivity of knowledge workers

Eric Matson and Laurence Prusak

The key is identifying and addressing the barriers workers face in their daily interactions.

Are you doing all that you can to enhance the productivity of your knowledge workers? It's a simple question, but one that few senior executives can answer.

Their confusion isn't for lack of trying. Organizations around the world struggle to crack the code for improving the effectiveness of managers, salespeople, scientists, and others whose jobs consist primarily of interactions—with other employees, customers, and suppliers—and complex decision making based on knowledge and judgment.[1] The stakes are high: raising the productivity of these workers, who constitute a large and growing share of the workforce in developed economies, represents a major opportunity for companies, as well as for countries with low birthrates that hope to maintain GDP growth.

Nonetheless, many executives have a hazy understanding of what it takes to bolster productivity for knowledge workers. This lack of clarity is partly because knowledge work involves more diverse and amorphous tasks than do production or clerical positions, where the relatively clear-cut, predictable activities make jobs easier to automate or streamline. Likewise, performance metrics are hard to come by in knowledge work, making it challenging to manage improvement efforts (which often lack a clear owner in the first place). Against this backdrop, it's perhaps unsurprising that many companies settle for scattershot investments in training and IT systems.

Since knowledge workers spend half their time on interactions, our research and experience suggest that companies should first explore the productivity barriers that impede these interactions. Armed with a better understanding of the constraints, senior executives can get more bang for their buck by identifying targeted productivity-improvement efforts to increase both the efficiency and effectiveness of the interactions between workers.

Among companies we've surveyed (see sidebar, "About the research"),

Knowledge workers make up more than **40 percent** of the US workforce.

fully half of all interactions are constrained by one of five barriers: physical, technical, social or cultural, contextual, and temporal. While individual companies will encounter some obstacles more than others, our experience suggests that the approaches to overcoming them are widely applicable.

Physical and technical barriers

Physical barriers (including geographic distance and differences in time zones) often go hand in hand with *technical* barriers because the lack of effective tools for locating the right people and collaborating becomes even more pronounced when they are far away. While these barriers are on the wane at many companies given the arsenal of software tools available, some large, globally dispersed organizations continue to suffer from them.

One remedy implemented by some organizations is to create "communities of practice" for people who could benefit from one another's advice—as the World Bank has done to help the 100 or so of its planners who focus on urban poverty to facilitate discussions on projects to upgrade slums. The communities feature online tools to help geographically dispersed members search for basic information (say, member roles and the specific challenges they are addressing) and sometimes use the latest social-networking tools to provide more sophisticated information, including whom the members have worked or trained with. By supplementing electronic tools with videoconferences and occasional in-person meetings, communities can bridge physical distances and build relationships.

Social or cultural barriers

Examples of *social* or *cultural* barriers include rigid hierarchy or ineffective incentives that don't spur the right people to engage. To avoid such problems, Petrobras, the Brazil-based oil major, created a series of case studies focused on real events in the company's past that illuminate its values, processes, and norms. The cases are discussed with new hires in small groups—promoting a better understanding of how the organization works and encouraging a culture of knowledge sharing and collaborative problem solving. (To benefit further from such approaches, companies should include knowledge sharing in performance reviews and ensure that team leaders clearly communicate acceptable response times for information requests. The communities of practice described above can help too: employees are far more likely to give timely and useful responses to people in their network.)

About the research

This article summarizes the results of a research project under way since 2006. In the first phase, more than 200 knowledge workers at four organizations—the research institute Battelle, Educational Testing Service (ETS), Novartis, and the US Defense Intelligence Agency—kept daily logs of their knowledge interactions (more than 3,000 in total). Subsequently, we conducted field research and interviews with about 35 people at the original four companies plus three new ones: Ecopetrol, NASA, and Petrobras. For more on the first phase of research, see Al Jacobson and Laurence Prusak, "The cost of knowledge," *Harvard Business Review*, November 2006.

Ecopetrol's technical forums break down the natural barriers between occupations and promote knowledge sharing across geographic boundaries.

© Oscar Javier Guerra Perdomo

Contextual barriers

Employees who face *contextual* barriers struggle to share and translate knowledge obtained from colleagues in different fields. Complex interactions often require contact with people in other departments or divisions, making it hard for workers to assess a colleague's level of expertise or apply the advice they may receive. Think of the disconnect that often occurs between a company's sales department and its product-development team over customer data. The two groups frequently struggle to communicate because they think and talk so differently about the subject (sales

staff devote attention to customer insights while developers focus on product specifications).

To overcome contextual barriers, organizations can rotate employees across teams and divisions or create forums where specialists in different areas can learn about one another's work. The US National Aeronautics and Space Administration (NASA), for instance, holds a biannual "Masters Forum" to share knowledge across disciplines. About 50 employees from different parts of the agency attend the meetings to hear other NASA colleagues talk about the tools, methods, and skills

NASA's biannual "Masters Forums," attended by about 50 employees from different parts of the agency, help transfer knowledge across disciplines. © Kerry Ellis/NASA

they use in extremely complex projects. The sessions are lightly moderated and very interactive.

Similarly, managers at Ecopetrol, a Colombian gas and oil company, have found that technical forums not only break down the natural barriers between occupations but also facilitate knowledge sharing across geographic boundaries. Moreover, the forums build trust, which encourages employees to share information more freely.

The barrier of time

The final barrier is *time*, or rather the perceived lack of it. If valuable interactions are falling victim to time constraints, executives can use job roles and responsibilities to help identify the employees that knowledge workers should be interacting with and on what topics. In some cases, companies may need to clarify decision rights and redefine roles to reduce the interaction burden on some employees while increasing it on others.

Boston-based Millennium Pharmaceuticals, which develops drugs for cancer treatment, did just that. When it found that researchers didn't have time to share lessons from their experiments, it created a small group of scientists to act as "knowledge intermediaries." Based on meetings with company scientists as well as presentations, these employees summarize findings and submit them to an internal database. They also act as brokers by sharing knowledge across groups. The company reckons that this practice, combined with other initiatives, has boosted success rates for the company's research and reduced the time needed to make key decisions. ○

[1]For this article, we define *knowledge interactions* as those involving only the knowledge in people's heads, not data or basic information that can be downloaded through technology alone.

Eric Matson is a consultant in McKinsey's Boston office; **Laurence Prusak** is a visiting scholar at the University of Southern California Marshall School of Business and a former senior adviser to McKinsey.

For more on knowledge worker productivity, see "The next revolution in interactions" and "Competitive advantage from better interactions," on mckinseyquarterly.com.

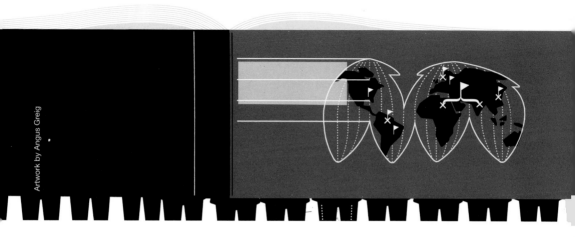

Artwork by Angus Greig

The right way to hedge

Bryan Fisher and Ankush Kumar

Hedging can generate financial, strategic, and operational benefits—but getting it wrong can destroy more value than was originally at risk.

Hedging is hot. Shifts in supply-and-demand dynamics and global financial turmoil have created unprecedented volatility in commodity prices in recent years. Meanwhile, executives at companies that buy, sell, or produce commodities have faced equally dramatic swings in profitability. Many have stepped up their use of hedging, in an attempt to manage this volatility and, in some instances, to avoid situations that could put a company's survival in jeopardy. Done well, the financial, strategic, and operational benefits of hedging can go beyond merely avoiding financial distress, by opening up options to preserve and create value as well.

Yet when done poorly, hedging in commodities often overwhelms the logic behind it and can actually destroy more value than was originally at risk—say, when individual business units hedge opposite sides of the same risk or managers expend too much effort hedging risks that are immaterial to a company's health. Managers can also underestimate the full costs of hedging or overlook operational or natural hedges in deference to costly financial ones. No question, hedging can entail complex calculations and difficult trade-offs. But in our experience, keeping in mind a few simple pointers can help nip problems early and make hedging strategies more effective.

For more on managing risk across the enterprise, see "The CEO's guide to corporate finance," on page 68.

Hedge net economic exposure

Too many hedging programs target the nominal risks of "siloed" business units or divisions rather than a company's net economic exposure—the aggregated risk across the enterprise. This fragmented approach is especially problematic in large organizations: managers of individual units focus on their own risks without considering risks and hedging activities elsewhere in the company.

At a large international industrial company, for example, one business unit decided to hedge its foreign-exchange exposure from the sale of $700 million in goods to Brazil. However, the unit's managers hadn't known that a second business unit was, meanwhile, sourcing about $500 million in goods from Brazil, so the company found itself with a net exposure of $500 million rather than the $200 million it naturally would have incurred by doing nothing.

Elsewhere, the purchasing manager of a large chemical company used the financial markets to hedge its more than $1 billion in direct natural-gas costs—half of its input costs for the year. However, the company's natural position had little exposure to gas price movements, since price fluctuations were already passed through to customers in its sales contracts.

Adding the financial hedge to its input costs had, in fact, significantly *increased* the company's exposure to natural-gas prices. Had the oversight gone unnoticed, a 20 percent decrease in gas prices would have wiped out all of the company's projected earnings.

Keep in mind that net economic exposure includes indirect risks, which can in some cases account for the bulk of a company's total risk exposure. Indirect risks arise from changes in business practices (say, contracting terms with customers) or market factors (such as changes in the competitive environment). For example, when a snowmobile manufacturer in Canada hedged the foreign-exchange exposure of its supply costs, denominated in Canadian dollars, it successfully protected itself from cost increases that resulted from the rise of the Canadian against the US dollar. However, the costs for the company's US competitors were in depreciating US dollars. The snowmobile maker's net economic exposure, therefore, came not just from higher manufacturing costs but also from lower sales as Canadian customers rushed to buy cheaper snowmobiles from competitors in the United States.

Many risk managers underestimate the true cost of hedging, typically focusing only on the direct transactional costs, such as bid–ask spreads and broker fees.

To identify a company's true economic exposure, start by determining the natural offsets across businesses to ensure that hedging activities don't actually increase it. Typically, identifying and aggregating exposure to risk on a company-wide basis involves compiling a global risk "book" (similar to those used by financial and other trading institutions) to see the big picture—the different elements of risk—on a consistent basis.

Calculate total costs and benefits

Many risk managers underestimate the true cost of hedging, typically focusing only on the direct transactional costs, such as bid–ask spreads and broker fees. These components are often only a small portion of total hedge costs, leaving out indirect ones, which can be the largest portion of the total. As a result, the cost of many hedging programs far exceeds their benefits.

Two kinds of indirect costs are worth examining: the opportunity cost of holding margin capital and lost upside. First, when a company enters into some financial-hedging arrangements, it often must hold additional capital on its balance sheet against potential future obligations. This requirement ties up capital that might have been better applied to other projects, creating an opportunity cost that managers often overlook.

The second indirect cost is lost upside. When the probability that prices will move favorably is higher than the probability that they'll move unfavorably, hedging to lock in current prices can cost more in forgone upside than the value of the downside protection. Of course, this cost depends on an organization's view of price floors and ceilings. A large independent natural-gas producer, for example, was evaluating a hedge for its production during the coming two years. The company's fundamental perspective was that gas prices in this period would stay within a range of $5.00 to $8.00 per million BTUs. Meanwhile, the price of natural gas in the futures markets was $5.50 per million BTUs. By hedging production at the prevailing futures market price, the company was guaranteeing itself revenue of $5.50 per million BTUs—$0.50 higher than the lowest price it thought plausible, but $2.50 lower than the highest.

Hedge only what matters

Companies should hedge only exposures that pose a material risk to their financial health or threaten their strategic plans. Yet too often we find that companies (under pressure from the capital markets) or individual business units (under pressure from management to provide earnings certainty) adopt hedging programs that create little or no value for shareholders. An integrated aluminum company, for example, hedged its exposure to crude oil and natural gas for years, even though these had a very limited impact on its overall margins. Large conglomerates are particularly susceptible to this pitfall when individual business units hedge to protect their performance against risks that are immaterial at a portfolio level. Hedging these smaller exposures affects a company's risk profile only marginally—and isn't worth the management time and focus such hedges require.

To determine whether exposure to a given risk is material, managers must determine whether a company's cash flows are adequate for its cash needs. Yet most managers base their assessments of cash flows on scenarios, without considering how likely those scenarios are. This approach is better than nothing, but it doesn't shed enough light on the company's true susceptibility to financial distress.

A more effective approach is to develop a profile of probable cash flows that reflects a company-wide calculation of risk exposures and sources of cash. To quantify the likelihood of a shortfall, managers can then compare the cash flow profile with the company's cash needs, starting with the least discretionary and moving to the most discretionary. They should be sure to conduct this analysis at the portfolio level to account for the diversification of risks across different business lines.

If the results show a high probability of a cash shortfall given non-discretionary cash requirements, such as debt obligations or maintenance capital expenditures, the company probably faces a high risk of financial distress. Companies in this position should take aggressive steps, including hedging, to mitigate risk. If, on the other hand, the analysis reveals that the company can finance its strategic plans with a high degree of certainty,

even absent hedging, it should avoid (or unwind) an expensive hedging program.

....

Look beyond financial hedges

Finally, risk managers shouldn't overlook combinations of financial hedges and nonfinancial levers to alleviate risk. Many companies fail to explore financial hedging's alternatives, which include commercial or operational tactics that can reduce risks more effectively and inexpensively. Among them: contracting decisions that pass risk through to a counterparty; strategic moves, such as vertical integration; and operational changes, such as revising product specifications, shutting down manufacturing facilities when input costs peak, or holding additional cash reserves. Companies should test the effectiveness of different risk mitigation strategies by quantitatively comparing the total cost of each approach with the benefits. ○

Bryan Fisher and **Ankush Kumar** are principals in McKinsey's Houston office.

The full version of this article is available on mckinseyquarterly.com.

Spotlight on training

Measuring the impact of training:
The Boys & Girls Clubs of America set the pace, page 108.

© Tom Merton/Getty Images

Getting more from your training programs

Aaron DeSmet, Monica McGurk, and Elizabeth Schwartz

To improve results from training programs, executives must focus on what happens in the workplace before and after employees go to class.

Companies around the world spend up to $100 billion a year[1] to train employees in the skills they need to improve corporate performance—topics like communication, sales techniques, performance management, or lean operations. But training typically doesn't have much impact. Indeed, only one-quarter of the respondents to a recent McKinsey survey said their training programs measurably improved business performance, and most companies don't even bother to track the returns they get on their investments in training.[2] They keep at it because a highly skilled workforce is clearly more productive and because employees often need new skills to deal with changes in an organization's strategy or performance.

Given how important skilled workers are, companies must do better at creating them. When senior leaders focus on making training work—and get personally involved—improvement can come rapidly. The content of the training itself is not the biggest issue, though many companies could certainly improve it. The most significant improvements lie in rethinking the mind-sets that employees and their leaders bring to training, as well as the environment they come back to afterward. These are tasks only senior leaders can take on.

For more on best practices in training, see the sidebar "Getting training content right," in the extended version of this article, on mckinseyquarterly.com.

Before training begins

1. Help people want to learn

Adults learn in predictable steps. Before employees can master a new skill effectively, for example, they must be convinced it will help improve their organization's performance, recognize that their own performance is weak in that area, and then actually *choose* to learn.[3] Yet most corporate training programs overlook these prerequisites and just assume that employees "get it." This approach is a big mistake because it allows normal patterns of skepticism to become barriers to learning. The results are familiar to anyone who has attended a corporate training event. Instead of approaching training as active learners, many employees behave as if they were prisoners ("I'm here because I have to be"), vacationers ("I don't mind being here—it's a nice break from doing real work"), or professors ("Everybody else is here to learn; I can just share my wisdom").

To avert these outcomes, companies must help employees to internalize the need for change and to develop the desire to gain the skills that will bring progress. The best method is to include trainees or their peers in determining what changes need to be made and why, thereby creating credible ambassadors for the effort. If this isn't possible, a similar purpose is served by beginning a training program with an analysis of the existing performance problems of the individuals or business units involved and of how the new skills will address these problems.

Consider the case of a retailer that knew its customer service and selling skills were relatively poor. In response, the company formed teams of district managers, customer service representatives, and salespeople to help it understand its current skill levels and to plan improvements. To observe good customer service, the teams visited high-performing organizations, such as the Ritz-Carlton. The teams also conducted mystery-shopping exercises, in which they did not reveal their corporate affiliations, at the stores of competitors, where they received mixed service at best, suggesting that service improvements could become a real competitive advantage. Teams also conducted exit surveys of the retailer's own customers to correlate the quality of their experience with how much they purchased and whether or not they intended to return to the

Companies should ferret out problematic mind-sets with the same rigor they put into diagnosing skill gaps.

store. And the teams observed hundreds of their colleagues in action—enough to believe that the company was not delivering a great customer experience and that change was necessary.

To improve customer service and selling, the teams then designed new processes and tools, including guidelines that helped salespeople translate product features into benefits that shoppers could relate to. Next, they began piloting the improvements at a few stores. The results were impressive—a double-digit leap in conversion rates and rising sales in important product categories. Better yet, after showcasing the results at a meeting of the company's retail managers and establishing the program's credibility, the teams found the managers clamoring for the chance to have training start at their stores.

2. Uncover harmful mind-sets

Even when employees *do* learn what they're taught, they very often don't apply it. If this happens, the training will be wasted—no matter how good it is. Preexisting mind-sets are one frequent cause of this problem. Companies should therefore ferret out problematic mind-sets with the same rigor they put into diagnosing skill gaps.

For instance, a big-box retailer had been trying to increase its focus on customers for more than two years. It invested millions of dollars in teaching a five-step selling process, monitoring customer feedback, and rolling out e-learning programs to improve its employees' knowledge of the products it sold. Salespeople passed every certification test they were given yet still didn't use the new skills on the floor. Customer feedback and store performance remained lackluster.

To figure out why, the company conducted a mix of employee interviews, focus groups, and surveys. Two troubling mind-sets emerged. First, salespeople fundamentally believed that the behavior of shoppers had shifted, so that they now primarily browsed in stores and made most purchases online. Thus, employees associated attending to shoppers with a low payoff. Second, salespeople clung to age, gender, and racial stereotypes about which customers would make purchases—and tended to ignore the others. An examination of shopper survey, purchase, and conversion data proved both mind-sets false.

The company relaunched its training efforts, now grounded in an open discussion of these two mind-sets, using facts to dispel the myths and to build new enthusiasm for customer service. Salespeople began to apply the methods they'd already learned, which quickly drove a 150-basis-point improvement in conversion rates at the pilot stores and a 20 percent improvement in their net income.

© Steve Dunwell/Corbis

One company's teams visited the Ritz-Carlton and other high-performing companies to observe good customer service.

3. Get the leaders on board

To ensure that the lessons stick when training ends, companies must have meaningful support from the relevant leaders beforehand. This point sounds obvious, but we've seen many training programs stall when leaders agree with program goals in principle yet fail to reflect them in their own behavior, thereby signaling to employees that change isn't necessary.

For example, one industrial company noted a need to upgrade the skills of its marketing department. The HR staff launched a well-conceived program—based on a clear definition of the new skills good marketers must have—that included a curriculum developed by a leading university. In parallel, the company hired several employees who had the skills it was trying to foster and who would,

presumably, help their colleagues develop them. After sending marketing staffers through the program, however, senior executives still expressed frustration with the department's capabilities. Worse, many marketers appeared to be spending time on things that weren't really marketing, such as resolving customer service breakdowns.

A closer examination revealed that the new marketing skills hadn't taken root, because the company hadn't trained the department's leaders, who lacked the necessary skills and could not be effective role models. Further, the leaders were not prepared to change the way they ran meetings, made decisions about branding or advertising programs, conducted performance dialogues, or coached others on marketing skills. Consequently, employees perceived that their bosses weren't particularly interested in having them apply the new skills and that they should continue to spend a significant amount of time on old activities, such as resolving customer crises.

Outcomes are much better when business leaders participate in the design and delivery of training programs and connect them to the new ways of working. For example, one consumer goods company hoping to bolster its marketing skills began by including senior managers from a range of functions in a detailed discussion about what marketing skills were needed. Marketing leaders then restructured the relevant processes—for instance, those related to generating customer insights—to leverage the program's content explicitly. To drive home the importance of implementing the new skills, company leaders went through the training first; many taught subsequent courses and also served as role models to reinforce the new behavior afterward. The program as a whole improved business performance tremendously, helping the company to shift from declining or flat unit volumes to double-digit volume growth and from stagnant net sales and operating-margin growth to a robust compound annual growth rate (CAGR) of 9 percent.

Back in the workplace

4. Reinforce the new skills

Participants rarely leave any training program entirely prepared to put new skills into practice. Old habits die hard, after all, so reinforcing and supporting new kinds of behavior after they are learned is crucial. Furthermore, companies typically expect employees to go back to work and figure out for themselves how to incorporate what they've learned into their day-to-day activities, which often take up all of their time as is.

This was a particular problem for a biotech company trying to beef up its poor performance-management skills. (Indeed, at the outset of the effort, performance management was so rudimentary that employees didn't even have job descriptions.) The company dedicated itself to improvement and trained all its managers in the necessary skills. But when those managers got back to work, they couldn't find the time to integrate performance reviews into their routines and got no help doing so. Two years later, nothing had changed, and all that the managers had learned was lost.

Contrast this experience with that of a large manufacturer also trying to improve its performance-management skills. The company had trained its frontline supervisors on coaching and on conducting better performance dialogues with line workers, and the supervisors had agreed to begin practicing the new skills immediately. The supervisors even had laminated cards they could use as "cheat sheets" to guide the conversations.

But back on the shop floor, a multitude of distractions, fires to fight, and other mundane barriers made it easy to slip back into old habits. In fact, a check-in later during the week when the training occurred revealed that the supervisors weren't practicing *any* of the new behavior. When company executives asked why, it became clear that the supervisors hadn't made the time—in part because the coaching and feedback conversations would be difficult but also because the supervisors felt management wouldn't support their efforts. Previous training exercises, the supervisors noted, had never been accompanied by follow-up.

To show that things would be different this time, the executives insisted that the conversations take place and even shadowed the supervisors on the shop floor to help them. While this was uncomfortable for everyone involved, the supervisors soon gained confidence using the new skills and began to see results. Indeed, within just two months, productivity, reliability, and safety performance had all improved, and the plant was able to produce 25 percent more output than it had in the past.

Prisoners or active learners? By motivating employees before training starts, companies can prevent normal patterns of skepticism from becoming barriers to learning in the classroom.

© Ryan McVay/Getty Images

5. Measure the impact

Measuring impact seems basic, but most companies simply don't do it. McKinsey research finds that only 50 percent of organizations even bother to keep track of participants' feedback about training programs. Worse, only 30 percent use any other kind of metric. What this means, of course, is that many companies essentially measure the effectiveness of training by asking the participants if they liked it. Besides the risk of encouraging "edutainment" over substance, the problem with this approach is that it penalizes programs that push people outside their comfort zones. What's more, it leaves HR departments and other developers of training programs flying blind about their impact. The solution, as we explain in a companion article on page 108, is to track the impact of training programs against whatever hard business metric they are meant to improve. If that's not possible, measuring leading-edge indicators, such as actual behavior change, can provide insights.

Training can go wrong in all kinds of ways. But the most important failures occur outside the classroom. By focusing on creating a receptive mind-set for training before it happens—and ensuring a supportive environment afterward—companies can dramatically improve the business impact of their training programs. ○

Aaron DeSmet is a principal in McKinsey's Houston office, **Monica McGurk** is a principal in the Atlanta office, and **Elizabeth Schwartz** is an associate principal in the New Jersey office.

[1] Bersin & Associates, figure for global spending, 2008.
[2] See "Building organizational capabilities: McKinsey Global Survey results," mckinseyquarterly.com, March 2010.
[3] See Malcolm S. Knowles, Elwood F. Holton III, and Richard A. Swanson, *The Adult Learner: The Definitive Classic in Adult Education and Human Resource Development*, sixth edition, London: Elsevier, 2005.

Case study:

The Boys & Girls Clubs of America put a value on training

Jenny Cermak and Monica McGurk

Few companies actually measure the value of their training programs. Surprisingly, it's a nonprofit that's leading the way.

Organizations typically measure the impact of their training programs by conducting surveys of attendees or counting how many employees complete courses rather than by assessing whether employees learned anything that improved business performance. This approach was, perhaps, acceptable when companies had money to spare. Now, most don't.

The story of one social-sector organization, the Boys & Girls Clubs of America (BGCA), illustrates how organizations can make the most of their outlays for training programs by understanding which ones create business value. The lessons are remarkably straightforward, and we believe they can be applied to retailers, manufacturers, and a range of other organizations as well.

For more on the state of corporate skill building, see "Building organizational capabilities: McKinsey Global Survey results," on mckinseyquarterly.com.

How the Boys & Girls Clubs measure training results

BGCA has the largest budget of any nonprofit in the United States. Some 1,100 local organizations manage their own resource development, strategic planning, programming, and fund-raising. They oversee 4,000 individual club locations that provide a place for young people to learn and participate in athletic and life skills programs.

The clubs faced a common problem: a lack of capabilities in a core area—leadership. A wave of retirements among senior managers had magnified the problem, which was further accentuated by a growth strategy aimed at expanding the number of club locations. BGCA leaders had to overcome an additional obstacle: donors were far more interested in supporting programs that benefited children directly rather than overhead, such as training. Therefore, it was imperative for BGCA to prove the performance impact of any training it undertook.

The organization began by conducting a 360-degree assessment of every local leader, employing a capability model that measured nearly 50 aspects of leadership. Regression analysis helped BGCA correlate each aspect of leadership with local organizational performance on crucial measures such as growth in membership and funds raised—measures that it already tracked to assess the organizations as a whole. Four out of the 50 aspects contributed disproportionately to performance: the leader's ability to build effective boards, pursue successful revenue-development strategies, use an investor's mind-set toward programs and resource development, and lead with tenacity and persistence.

BGCA therefore built its training program around those four subjects. The program involved both intensive classroom work and a project chosen by each local team, ranging from implementing new HR processes to deepening the impact of after-school programs. By the end of 2009, more than 650 leaders from approximately 250 local organizations had been trained.

Because the program was designed to raise specific organizational-performance outcomes, the process of assessing its impact was straightforward: compare the results from local organizations whose leaders had received training with those whose leaders hadn't. The downturn in the economy, as well as preexisting economic differences among cities, complicated efforts to assess gains in membership and fund-raising on an absolute basis. However, by carefully pairing local organizations that had participated

in training with those that hadn't, BGCA was able to screen out the impact of external factors (for example, unemployment or differences in local educational-attainment rates) on membership and fund-raising. In this way, BGCA could isolate the effect of training itself. BGCA also surveyed local board members before and after training to assess leaders' changes in behavior related to board leadership.

On average, locations where the leaders had been trained bested the control group on every performance outcome measured. If all 1,100 BGCA member organizations reached that level of success, BGCA would see more than 350,000 new members and more than $100 million in annual incremental revenue—a 2 to 3 percent increase in the average location's budget, a meaningful sum at a time of precarious funding. Moreover, BGCA determined that it generated more than a fourfold return on costs for the program, even when including the imputed cost of participants' time, as well as travel and training expenses (Exhibit 1).

BGCA then compared performance among participants (Exhibit 2) and found that the gains of participants in the highest quartile were significantly higher than the average. The high performers typically focused on very aspirational projects; set clear, quantifiable goals; and took the extra step of teaching what they had learned to the rest of their organization. Those insights led BGCA to adjust the training curriculum to reinforce the success factors.

Applying the lessons

Companies have an advantage in applying the above lessons. Most for-profit organizations have a longer list of quantitative performance metrics than BGCA does. But most don't use them to measure the impact of their training efforts. A retailer pursuing better customer service and sales growth, for example, could train employees on best-practice customer-engagement techniques. Rather than just measuring employee satisfaction with the training, the percentage of employees actually taking the training, or "pass rates" on training exams, the retailer should measure the impact of its programs through hard business

---

Exhibit 1

A big payoff: BGCA's returns from training are at least four times the investment.

Estimated impact of Boys & Girls Clubs of America (BGCA) training program

Impact of advanced-leadership program on revenues, $ million	÷	Cost of advanced-leadership program, $ million	=	Return on investment (ROI)
Increase, 2008–09 — 30–35		All-in cost, 2007–09 — 7.3		4–5x
Future annual increase — 15–20		Future annual cost — 2.5		6–8x

Source: BGCA; McKinsey analysis

Exhibit 2

Back on the job: Top-quartile trainees made significant advances.

Boys & Girls Clubs of America (BGCA) training attendees' performance before and after training

Difference between performance gains of highest-quartile training participants[1] and average ones, 2009 vs 2007, percentage points

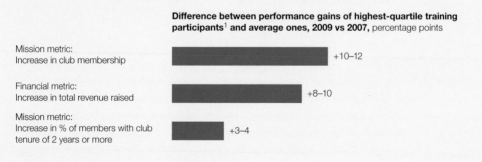

Mission metric: Increase in club membership	+10–12
Financial metric: Increase in total revenue raised	+8–10
Mission metric: Increase in % of members with club tenure of 2 years or more	+3–4

[1] Defined as 75th percentile.

Source: BGCA; McKinsey analysis

metrics, such as sales, basket size, and conversion rates in critical categories or departments. Similarly, a manufacturer might try to improve its operations by teaching plant supervisors lean-manufacturing and coaching skills, but rather than tracking only how many managers have been trained, it should track metrics such as downtime, the overall effectiveness of equipment, or fill rates.

In every case, companies must continually review and revise the links between skills, performance, and training programs. Typically, to determine which metrics should be improved, companies assess their current performance against either industry benchmarks or their own goals. Like retailers or manufacturers, most companies know what kinds of skills are tied to different areas of performance. So a good next step is to conduct an analysis of relevant employee groups to identify the most important specific skills for them (as BGCA did) and which performance-enhancing skills they currently lack. To get a clear read on the impact of a program, it's crucial to control for the influence of external factors (such as the opening of new retail competitors in local markets) as well as the impact of extraordinary internal factors (such as a scheduled plant shutdown for preventative maintenance). It's also crucial to make appropriate comparisons within peer groups defined by preexisting performance bands or market types.

• • •

By tying the curricula of training more closely to key performance metrics and then measuring its impact against them, organizations can generate greater value from training programs and find useful insights to improve them constantly. ○

Jenny Cermak is a consultant in McKinsey's Atlanta office, where **Monica McGurk** is a principal.

Extra Point

The four cornerstones of corporate finance

In a new book, *Value: The Four Cornerstones of Corporate Finance*, McKinsey's Richard Dobbs, Bill Huyett, and Tim Koller show the power of four disarmingly simple but often-ignored financial principles. Here are some practical applications.

In practice:
Evaluating projects

A company shouldn't pass up potentially high-return projects just because they have moderate downside risk.

In practice:
Mergers and acquisitions

Be wary of mergers that are justified (or vetoed) on the basis of their impact on earnings per share. Earnings per share (EPS) has nothing to say about how merging two entities will change the cash flows they generate.

Core-of-value principle:

Value creation is driven by growth and returns on capital.

Conservation-of-value principle:

You can't create value by rearranging claims on cash flows.

Value creation

Expectations treadmill principle:

The more investors expect of your share price, the better you must perform to keep up.

Best-owner principle:

A business's value depends upon its owner's capabilities.

In practice:
Executive compensation

Emphasize long-term growth and returns on capital improvements, measure performance against market expectations, and index compensation to the market performance of peer companies.

In practice:
Divestitures

A multibusiness company should regularly hold business-exit reviews and place a date stamp on divisions, with a milestone for assessing whether it is still the best owner.

For more on these financial principles and their application to everyday business decisions, see Dobbs, Huyett, and Koller's article, "The CEO's guide to corporate finance," on page 68.